MACAT

An Analysis of

Milton Friedman's

The Role of
Monetary Policy

T0301891

John Collins
with
Nick Broten

Published by Macat International Ltd
24:13 Coda Centre, 189 Munster Road, London SW6 6AW.

Distributed exclusively by Routledge
2 Park Square, Milton Park, Abingdon, Oxon OX14 4RN
711 Third Avenue, New York, NY 10017, USA

Routledge is an imprint of the Taylor & Francis Group, an informa business

www.macat.com
info@macat.com

Cataloguing in Publication Data
A catalogue record for this book is available from the British Library.
Library of Congress Cataloguing-in-Publication Data is available upon request.
Cover illustration: Etienne Gilfillan

ISBN 978-1-912302-21-5 (hardback)
ISBN 978-1-912127-36-8 (paperback)
ISBN 978-1-912281-09-1 (e-book)

Notice
The information in this book is designed to orientate readers of the work under analysis,
to elucidate and contextualise its key ideas and themes, and to aid in the development
of critical thinking skills. It is not meant to be used, nor should it be used, as a
substitute for original thinking or in place of original writing or research. References and
notes are provided for informational purposes and their presence does not constitute
endorsement of the information or opinions therein. This book is presented solely for
educational purposes. It is sold on the understanding that the publisher is not engaged
to provide any scholarly advice. The publisher has made every effort to ensure that
this book is accurate and up-to-date, but makes no warranties or representations with
regard to the completeness or reliability of the information it contains. The information
and the opinions provided herein are not guaranteed or warranted to produce particular
results and may not be suitable for students of every ability. The publisher shall not be
liable for any loss, damage or disruption arising from any errors or omissions, or from
the use of this book, including, but not limited to, special, incidental, consequential or
other damages caused, or alleged to have been caused, directly or indirectly, by the
information contained within.

CONTENTS

THE MACAT LIBRARY

The Macat Library is a series of unique academic explorations of seminal works in the humanities and social sciences – books and papers that have had a significant and widely recognised impact on their disciplines. It has been created to serve as much more than just a summary of what lies between the covers of a great book. It illuminates and explores the influences on, ideas of, and impact of that book. Our goal is to offer a learning resource that encourages critical thinking and fosters a better, deeper understanding of important ideas.

Each publication is divided into three Sections: Influences, Ideas, and Impact. Each Section has four Modules. These explore every important facet of the work, and the responses to it.

This Section-Module structure makes a Macat Library book easy to use, but it has another important feature. Because each Macat book is written to the same format, it is possible (and encouraged!) to cross-reference multiple Macat books along the same lines of inquiry or research. This allows the reader to open up interesting interdisciplinary pathways.

To further aid your reading, lists of glossary terms and people mentioned are included at the end of this book (these are indicated by an asterisk [*] throughout) – as well as a list of works cited.

Macat has worked with the University of Cambridge to identify the elements of critical thinking and understand the ways in which six different skills combine to enable effective thinking.
Three allow us to fully understand a problem; three more give us the tools to solve it. Together, these six skills make up the **PACIER** model of critical thinking. They are:

ANALYSIS – understanding how an argument is built
EVALUATION – exploring the strengths and weaknesses of an argument
INTERPRETATION – understanding issues of meaning

CREATIVE THINKING – coming up with new ideas and fresh connections
PROBLEM-SOLVING – producing strong solutions
REASONING – creating strong arguments

To find out more, visit **WWW.MACAT.COM.**

CRITICAL THINKING AND "THE ROLE OF MONETARY POLICY"

Primary critical thinking skill: EVALUATION
Secondary critical thinking skill: REASONING

Milton Friedman was one of the most influential economists of all time – and his ideas had a huge impact on the economic policies of governments across the world.

A key theorist of capitalism and its relationship to democratic freedoms, Friedman remains one of the most cited authorities in both academic economics and government economic policy. His work remains striking not just for its brilliant grasp of economic laws and realities, but also for its consistent application of high-level evaluation and reasoning skills to produce arguments that can convince experts and laypeople alike.

Friedman's 1968 essay 'The Role of Monetary Policy' is a key example of how Friedman's critical thinking skills helped to cement his influence and reputation. The paper addressed the question of how a government's monetary policy affects the economy – from employment levels to inflation and so on. At its heart lies an evaluation and critique of the most widely accepted conception of monetary policy at the time – the 'Phillips Curve' – which argued that increased inflation leads naturally to increased employment. Systematically noting the flaws and weaknesses of the Phillips Curve theory, Friedman showed why this is not, in fact, the case. He then drew up a systematic alternative argument for what governmental monetary policy could and should aim to do.

Though economists now consider Friedman's ideas to have considerable limitations, 'The Role of Monetary Policy' remains a masterclass in evaluating and countering faulty arguments.

ABOUT THE AUTHOR OF THE ORIGINAL WORK

The son of Jewish immigrants from eastern Europe, economist **Milton Friedman** was born in New York City in 1912. He came of age during the Great Depression of the 1930s, an experience that helped shape his outlook for the rest of his life. In 1946, Friedman joined the faculty at the University of Chicago to teach economic theory, and eventually became a leading promoter of its free-market ideas. He advised President Reagan and Prime Minister Thatcher in the 1980s, wrote about a wide range of economics issues, and won the Nobel Prize in Economics for his body of work. He died in 2006 at the age of 94.

ABOUT THE AUTHORS OF THE ANALYSIS

Nick Broten was educated at the California Institute of Technology and the London School of Economics. He is doing postgraduate work at the Pardee RAND Graduate School and works as an assistant policy analyst at RAND. His current policy interests include designing distribution methods for end-of-life care, closing labour market skill gaps, and understanding biases in risk-taking by venture capitalists.

Dr John Collins is a member of the faculty at the London School of Economics, where he is currently Executive Director of the LSE IDEAS International Drug Policy Project.

ABOUT MACAT

GREAT WORKS FOR CRITICAL THINKING

Macat is focused on making the ideas of the world's great thinkers accessible and comprehensible to everybody, everywhere, in ways that promote the development of enhanced critical thinking skills.

It works with leading academics from the world's top universities to produce new analyses that focus on the ideas and the impact of the most influential works ever written across a wide variety of academic disciplines. Each of the works that sit at the heart of its growing library is an enduring example of great thinking. But by setting them in context – and looking at the influences that shaped their authors, as well as the responses they provoked – Macat encourages readers to look at these classics and game-changers with fresh eyes. Readers learn to think, engage and challenge their ideas, rather than simply accepting them.

'Macat offers an amazing first-of-its-kind tool for interdisciplinary learning and research. Its focus on works that transformed their disciplines and its rigorous approach, drawing on the world's leading experts and educational institutions, opens up a world-class education to anyone.'

Andreas Schleicher
Director for Education and Skills, Organisation for Economic Co-operation and Development

'Macat is taking on some of the major challenges in university education … They have drawn together a strong team of active academics who are producing teaching materials that are novel in the breadth of their approach.'

Prof Lord Broers,
former Vice-Chancellor of the University of Cambridge

'The Macat vision is exceptionally exciting. It focuses upon new modes of learning which analyse and explain seminal texts which have profoundly influenced world thinking and so social and economic development. It promotes the kind of critical thinking which is essential for any society and economy. This is the learning of the future.'

Rt Hon Charles Clarke, former UK Secretary of State for Education

'The Macat analyses provide immediate access to the critical conversation surrounding the books that have shaped their respective discipline, which will make them an invaluable resource to all of those, students and teachers, working in the field.'

Professor William Tronzo, University of California at San Diego

WAYS IN TO THE TEXT

KEY POINTS

- Milton Friedman was a Nobel Prize*-winning American economist and one of the twentieth century's most influential economic thinkers. He made key contributions to consumer theory (the analysis of sales and purchases), monetary economics* (the understanding of what happens when a government controls the amount of money available in an economy), and economic methodology (the methods used to study economics).
- Friedman's essay "The Role of Monetary Policy" outlines the problems with the monetary policy widely followed in the 1950s and 1960s and highlights the dangers of governments using the money supply* and interest rates* to try to adjust economic growth* and unemployment.*
- The essay was one of the most important economic policymaking texts of the twentieth century and a foundational piece in the school of monetarism*—the viewpoint that there can be advantages to adjusting the amount of money in circulation in an economy.

Who Was Milton Friedman?

Milton Friedman (1912–2006), the author of "The Role of Monetary Policy," was one of the most influential economists of all time. During his long and productive academic career, he made major contributions to the fields of macroeconomics* (the understanding of what an economy is and how it functions on the large scale), consumption theory* (roughly, the theory of sales and purchases), the methodology of economics (the methods used to study economics), and economic history.

Beyond his academic work, Friedman was known as an avid supporter of free-market* economics and individual liberty. His public lectures and publications, particularly the books *Capitalism and Freedom* (1962) and *Free to Choose* (1980), presented his libertarian* beliefs—freedom for the individual and minimal government interference—to a large audience and helped popularize free-market thinking.

Friedman was born in 1912 in New York City in the United States to first-generation Jewish* immigrants from Eastern Europe. Although his parents were not rich, they instilled in him a sense of ambition and self-reliance. Friedman graduated from Rutgers University in the state of New Jersey in 1932, during the catastrophic economic collapse known as the Great Depression.* The effects of this recession, both economic and intellectual, would inform his entire career. Of this time, Friedman says: "Though 1932–33, my first year at Chicago, was, financially, my most difficult year, intellectually, it opened new worlds ...."[1]

After obtaining a Master's in Economics from the University of Chicago in 1933, Friedman completed his PhD in Economics at Columbia University in 1946. That year, he began teaching full-time at the University of Chicago.

Friedman's relationship with the University of Chicago is a notable part of the impact he had. He was a key member of the "Chicago school of economics"*—a group of scholars associated with the university who shared a common belief that governments should not intervene in an economy, and a common interest in price theory.* According to price theory, the value of a thing depends on the relationship between supply (how easy that thing is to obtain) and demand (how much that thing is wanted).

The Chicago school is also associated with the monetarist approach to macroeconomic policy—that is, economic policy for the economy as a whole. Friedman lays out many parts of this policy in "The Role of Monetary Policy."

Friedman's association with the Chicago school has both supported and hurt his reputation. On the one hand, as one of the school's leading voices, it is likely that he was able to reach a larger audience than he would have through his academic work alone. On the other hand, the school, along with its most vocal promoters, has been a frequent target of left-wing* critics such as the Canadian author and activist Naomi Klein,* who oppose the free-market ideology it supports.[2]

What Does "The Role of Monetary Policy" Say?

Published in 1968, "The Role of Monetary Policy" was a challenge to the position that monetary policy (that is, a government's decision to increase or limit the amount of money available in an economy) is an effective tool for achieving long-term targets for inflation* and unemployment. That position was promoted by the so-called Keynesian* economists, who agreed with the English economist John Maynard Keynes* (1883–1846) that government spending on things such as public works benefitted the economy as a whole by stimulating employment, demand, and economic growth. This was the most widely accepted approach to economics when Friedman's book first appeared.

Friedman had a specific target in mind: the Phillips Curve,* a theory presented by William Phillips,* an economist from New Zealand, that suggests a negative relationship between inflation and unemployment. The theory states, in other words, that when inflation increases, unemployment will fall, and vice versa.

The promise of the Phillips Curve, which was fully worked out by the American economists Paul Samuelson* and Robert Solow* in 1960, is that monetary policy could be used as an instrument to achieve desired economic outcomes. If, for example, the monetary authority (generally a country's central bank) wanted to decrease unemployment, it could do so by increasing the money supply, which would drive up inflation as more money chases after the same amount of goods. So inflation and unemployment are trade-offs.

Friedman did not entirely agree, seeing this view of monetary policy as far too optimistic. It failed to take into account, he believed, that if people expect prices or wages to change, they change their behavior, and it ignored the crucial difference between real values* and nominal values.* While *nominal* values are simply the stated value of a good or a service, *real* values take into account price changes over time. For example: suppose your nominal wage is ten dollars per hour. If after every year the nominal wage stays the same but the cost of living goes up, then your real wage will actually fall over time. Friedman applies this idea to the Phillips Curve.

Suppose the monetary authority wants to decrease unemployment. According to the Phillips Curve, it can do so by increasing inflation. Due to the fact that the selling prices of goods tend to increase faster than nominal wages (the actual amount on workers' paychecks), this will drive down real wages. However, after a while this will cause employees to demand higher wages or drop out of the labor force. Unemployment then rises to its previous level. Friedman calls that rate the "natural rate of unemployment," and assumes it is more or less stable.[3]

He concludes this analysis by saying: "[The monetary authority] cannot use its control over nominal quantities to peg a real quantity—the real rate of interest, the rate of unemployment, the level of real national income, the real quantity of money, the rate of growth of the real national income, or the rate of growth of the real quantity of money."[4] In other words, Friedman shows that while the Phillips

Curve may hold in the short run, in the long run it will reverse, and thus policymakers are unwise to follow a policy based on it.

While much of Friedman's paper is concerned with the limitations of monetary policy, he concludes with suggestions for what policymakers can and should do. Most importantly, he suggests the goal of monetary policy should be to provide a steady money base for the economy in order to manage expectations and avoid unexpected shocks. Specifically, this means "adopting publicly the policy of achieving a steady rate of growth in a specified monetary total."[5] In other words, Friedman is not so much concerned with the actual level of the economy's money supply (the amount of money available). His concern is that the money supply should increase at a constant rate and that its increase is transparent.[6]

This rule of a steady increase of the money supply was central to monetary policy for more than a decade following the publication of Friedman's paper.

Why Does "The Role of Monetary Policy" Matter?

Although it is only 17 pages long, "The Role of Monetary Policy" is a key text in economics. The paper paved the way for the widespread adoption of the monetarist approach to macroeconomics and the impact of this is felt to this day. But it also predicted economic problems years before they actually occurred. As Friedman said himself, there was not "any doubt" that the essay's influence was helped by the fact that it predicted many of the economic problems that would plague Western economies during the 1970s.[7] For this reason, "The Role" is considered one of the most influential papers from one of the greatest economists of the twentieth century.

When we read the paper, we directly confront the central issues of monetary policy: What can adjusting the size of the money supply do? How effective is it? And what are the most useful policy goals?

While some of Friedman's answers to these questions are no longer considered correct, it is still valuable to follow his thinking. It is important to learn to think about questions such as the way changes in the money supply can lead to changes in the level of employment and prices. If we do, we can develop a deeper view of current events such as the controversies that raged over America's central bank, the Federal Reserve,* and its approach to the financial crisis of 2008–2010. The disagreements then revolved around the question of how effective monetary policy can be in returning the economy to a healthy state, particularly in times of crisis—the same question that Friedman addressed in his paper.[8]

Beyond the specific economic lessons in the paper, "The Role" is a wonderful example of logical reasoning. Reading it, students across the academic disciplines will gain an excellent lesson in how a widely held, but possibly misguided, position can be taken apart. Friedman's approach here, and one he often takes in his papers, is to follow each idea of his intellectual opponent to its logical end. In this case, he describes how the Phillips Curve may operate in the short term, but then shows how over time it will be reversed. This kind of argument forces the reader to challenge his or her beliefs and ideas—and offers an opportunity to grow.

NOTES

1   Milton Friedman, "Autobiography," *Nobel Prize in Economics*, accessed May 12, 2013, http://www.nobelprize.org/nobel_prizes/economics/laureates/1976/friedman-autobio.html.

2   Naomi Klein, *The Shock Doctrine: The Rise of Disaster Capitalism* (Toronto: Knopf Canada, 2009).

3   Milton Friedman, "The Role of Monetary Policy," *American Economic Review* 58, no. 1 (March 1, 1968): 8.

4   Friedman, "The Role": 11.

5   Friedman, "The Role": 16.

6   Friedman, "The Role": 17.

7   Quoted in Brian Snowdon and Howard R. Vane, *Modern Macroeconomics: Its Origins, Development and Current State* (Cheltenham: Edward Elgar, 2005), 204.

8   Stephen Williamson, "Kocherlakota: A Puzzle," accessed February 18, 2015, http://newmonetarism.blogspot.com/2013/09/kocherlakota-puzzle.html.

SECTION 1
INFLUENCES

MODULE 1
THE AUTHOR AND THE HISTORICAL CONTEXT

KEY POINTS

- "The Role of Monetary Policy" touches on a question of huge importance for policymakers. What role, if any, should government—specifically a government's monetary policy*—play in managing the economy?

- Growing up during the Great Depression* left a strong mark on Friedman. He attacked the Keynesian* analysis of the depression. For him, bad monetary policy contributed to the crash.

- The work was written after World War II* when economic policy was under debate. Some argued for central economic planning and strong government intervention, following the Keynesian tradition. Others argued for minimal government intervention as advocated by the "classical" economic tradition.*

Why Read This Text?

Milton Friedman's paper "The Role of Monetary Policy" is a key contribution to macroeconomics*—the study of the economy as a whole—and a short, clear statement of the monetarist* position within that field.

Monetarism was developed in the middle of the twentieth century, mainly by Friedman. It was opposed to the assumption, then widely accepted, that a government can improve the economy by adjusting the size of a country's supply of money—an idea promoted by the followers of the great British economist John Maynard Keynes.*

> ❝ Friedman always insisted that the greatest contribution he and his colleagues made to the revival of classical economic theory and practice lay not in their skill at promoting ideas but in their academic rigor and expertise. Within the profession, even those highly critical of Friedman's policy preferences recognized his brilliance and scholarly proficiency. ❞
>
> Lanny Ebenstein, in a review of *Milton Friedman: A Biography*

According to monetarism, this may work in the short run. But in the long run any positive effects such as greater employment will disappear and the attempt will cause more harm than good. The government's main task, said the monetarists, should be to adjust money supply* to keep prices stable.

Originally written as a speech to the American Economic Association in 1967, it had a deep and immediate impact on the attitude of economists towards monetary policy. The speech and the paper that followed it are one of several works that shifted mainstream opinion among economists and policymakers away from the Keynesian position and towards the monetarist position that then held sway in the 1970s.

Friedman's goal was to outline his vision for an effective monetary policy that would help achieve economic stability. For him, stability meant "high employment, stable prices and rapid growth."[1] The title he chose for his address was clear. "The Role of Monetary Policy" argued that monetary policy had a vital role to play in economic policymaking, but that its role and mechanisms were widely misunderstood. Specifically, Friedman argued that the Keynesian economists of the 1950s and 1960s misunderstood the relationship between inflation* and unemployment,* believing that governments could decrease unemployment by allowing inflation to happen. This belief came from an analysis of the Phillips Curve,* a formula that showed a "negative statistical link" between the two variables. In other words, it suggested that if you allow inflation to increase, this will reduce unemployment. Friedman showed with precise logic that this relationship applied, but only for so long. In the long run, he argued, it did not work.

Author's Life

Milton Friedman was born in 1912 in New York City to Jewish* immigrants from Eastern Europe.[2] He described his family as "a rather low-income family that had no particular understanding of the broader world."[3] It is likely that the economic uncertainty of his childhood and early adulthood, at the time of the Great Depression, influenced his approach to economics. In particular, during his early years Friedman developed a strong belief in the "basic forces of enterprise, ingenuity, invention, hard work, and thrift that are the true springs of economic growth."[4]

Although this philosophical orientation is more apparent in some of Friedman's other works, it is relevant to an understanding of "The Role," too. Friedman's challenge to the widely-accepted Keynesian approach to monetary policy is in some ways a call to be more humble about what government can accomplish in terms of improving the economy.

Friedman graduated from Rutgers University in New Jersey in 1932. He specialized in mathematics and was offered two scholarships to do graduate studies: one in mathematics at Brown University and one in economics at the University of Chicago. He chose economics, he recalled later, because the depression made economics seem a more important field of study at the time. He got his MA in Economics from the University of Chicago in 1933 and went on to earn his PhD from Columbia University, New York, in 1946. He then moved back to the University of Chicago, where he continued to teach until his retirement in 1977.[5] He remained active in the field of public policy until his death in 2006.

Throughout his career, both in academia and public debates, Friedman showed an interest in challenging accepted wisdom. And he stayed in the public eye. For example, his much-cited book *A Monetary History of the United States*, co-authored with the economist Anna Schwartz,* was a direct attack against the generally held view about the causes of the Great Depression. In particular, Friedman argued against the position that monetary policy had nothing to do with the crash.[6]

Friedman's attack was so influential that, in 2002, it inspired Ben Bernanke,* then a governor of the Federal Reserve* (one of seven members of the board of governors who oversee America's central bank), to declare: "Regarding the Great Depression. You're right, we did it. We're very sorry. But thanks to you, we won't do it again."[7]

Author's Background

The key economic event of the twentieth century, and a crucial event in the development of later economic thinking and policy, was the Great Depression. It left the American economy shrunken from the stock-market* crash of 1929 to the onset of World War II and had long-lasting effects around the globe. The "laboratory of the depression" is where many of Keynes's key ideas were developed, and most macroeconomists of the twentieth century in some way worked on dealing with that great slump. In 1995 Bernanke wrote: "To understand the Great Depression is the holy grail of macroeconomics."[8]

For Friedman, the impact of the depression was both intellectual and personal. His early life was shaped by the economic turmoil of the period, and his studies took place in the context of economic insecurity. As he writes: "It was taken for granted that I would attend college, though, also, that I would have to finance myself. I was awarded a competitive scholarship to Rutgers University … I was graduated from Rutgers in 1932, financing the rest of my college expenses by the usual mixture of waiting on tables, clerking in a retail store, occasional entrepreneurial ventures, and summer earnings."[9] With economic catastrophe as his backdrop, Friedman began his academic career in 1932 convinced of the importance of personal initiative over other sources of economic support—an attitude that can be readily seen in "The Role."

NOTES

1   Milton Friedman, "The Role of Monetary Policy," *American Economic Review* 58, no. 1 (March 1, 1968): 1.

2   Lanny Ebenstein, *Milton Friedman: A Biography* (Basingstoke: Palgrave Macmillan, 2007), 5–12.

3   Brian Snowdon and Howard R. Vane, *Modern Macroeconomics: Its Origins, Development and Current State* (Cheltenham: Edward Elgar, 2005), 199.

4   Friedman, "The Role": 17.

5   Snowdon and Vane, *Modern Macroeconomics*, 198–9.

6   Milton Friedman and Anna J. Schwartz, *A Monetary History of the United States, 1867–1960* (Princeton, NJ: Princeton University Press, 1963).

7   Ben Bernanke, "Remarks," accessed February 18, 2015, http://www.federalreserve.gov/boarddocs/Speeches/2002/20021108/default.htm.

8   Ben Bernanke, "The Macroeconomics of the Great Depression: A Comparative Approach," *Journal of Credit, Money, and Banking* 27, no. 1 (February 1995): 1.

9   Milton Friedman, "Autobiography," *Nobel Prize in Economics*, accessed May 12, 2013, http://www.nobelprize.org/nobel_prizes/economics/laureates/1976/friedman-autobio.html.

MODULE 2
ACADEMIC CONTEXT

KEY POINTS

- The study of economics is generally divided into two parts: microeconomics*—which looks at the actions of individuals and firms—and macroeconomics*—which looks at the whole economy of a country. Friedman's work is part of the latter group.

- Since the Keynesian* revolution of the 1930s and World War II,* governments and central banks around the world had moved uniformly away from classical economics (according to which an economy is self-regulating) towards policies of more active economic management.

- Friedman was part of the classical economic tradition,* which rejected ideas of government intervention in favor of free-market* capitalism.*

The Work in its Context

Milton Friedman's paper "The Role of Monetary Policy" discusses economics: the study of the production, distribution, and consumption of goods in society.

According to a famous definition of the subject from the British economist Lionel Robbins,* economics is "the science which studies human behavior as a relationship between given ends and scarce means which have alternative uses."[1] Although Robbins's definition captures the importance of scarcity* in economics, it does not quite show the breadth of the subject. Economics is generally divided into two streams: microeconomics and macroeconomics.

Microeconomics is the study of economic life at the level of

> **❝** If the Treasury were to fill old bottles with banknotes, bury them … and leave it to private enterprise on well-tried principles of laissez-faire* to dig the notes up … there need be no more unemployment. **❞**
>
> John Maynard Keynes, *The General Theory*

individuals and companies. It investigates such questions as how individuals make decisions about consumption and how firms set prices. Macroeconomics, the subject of "The Role of Monetary Policy," is the study of the economy as a whole.

Rather than looking at specific firms or people within the economy, macroeconomists study economic life at the national, regional, and global levels. To do so, they use economic indicators* and other variables such as gross national product* (the value of all the goods and services inside a country's borders at a certain time, sometimes called "gross domestic product"), the unemployment* rate, the exchange rate,* the growth rate,* the interest rate,* and the price level.*

It is worth noting that while these indicators are national or regional variables, Robbins's definition highlights the role of the individual in economics. While changes in interest rates, for example, may make individuals change their behavior, macroeconomists are only interested in behavioral changes that can be shown to operate on a larger scale.

Overview of the Field

Modern economics can be traced to the work of the Scottish political economist Adam Smith* and his book *An Inquiry into the Nature and Causes of the Wealth of Nations* (1776).[2] The model of capitalism* it presents is still relevant today.

Wealth of Nations is in many ways a book about free markets. Writing at a time when "mercantilist"* economic policies (prohibiting trade between nations) were dominant, Smith developed a clear theory that showed how free trade* and the division of labor* (both within a country and between nations) could benefit society.

Smith saw markets as natural to human life. He believed the inclination to "truck, barter, and trade one thing for another"— in other words, to freely exchange goods in a marketplace—was universal.[3] Perhaps most importantly, Smith described an economy in which individuals, acting in their immediate self-interest, produced the best outcomes for society. His famous concept of the "invisible hand" captures this idea: when individuals make decisions to maximize their own well-being, the forces of the market, which he calls the invisible hand, will guide those decisions towards the best outcomes.[4] As Smith writes, referring to an anonymous economic actor (that is, anyone participating in the economy at any level), "by pursuing his own interest he frequently promotes that of the society more effectually than when he really intends to promote it."[5]

While Smith is associated with supporting free markets, many of the famous economists to follow him were critical. Karl Marx's* *Das Kapital* (1867), for example, was a radical critique of free-market capitalism based on the idea that markets led to a concentration of wealth in the hands of capitalists.[6] Marx writes: "Within the capitalist system all methods for raising the social productiveness of labor are brought about at the cost of the individual laborer."[7]

While to a degree Smith saw markets as self-correcting, Marx saw them as engines of inequality between those who owned capital and those who worked for wages.

Another key work in economics is John Maynard Keynes's* *General Theory of Employment, Interest and Money* (1936), which offered a new support for government interventions to stimulate the economy. A central part of Keynes's theory is the idea of aggregate demand.* This is the total demand for goods and services in an economy—or, as Keynes puts it, an economic force that "relates various hypothetical quantities of employment to the proceeds which their outputs are expected to yield."[8]

The idea is vague on purpose. Keynesians believe aggregate demand can be "influenced by a host of economic decisions—both public and private—and sometimes behaves erratically,"[9] meaning somewhat randomly.

Keynesians also believe that when demand falls, bringing the threat of recession, government intervention in the form of fiscal stimulus*—that is, increased government spending on roads, education, the military, and so on—can bring the economy back to its productive potential.

Academic Influences

Friedman did not write "The Role" in an intellectual vacuum. In fact, the paper is widely associated with the Chicago school of economics,* whose guiding idea is the price theory.* At its most basic, price theory holds that in a free market the value of a good or service is determined by the relation between supply and demand, and shown by its price. A simple example is the water and diamonds paradox.

Water has an enormous economic benefit—life depends on it. Diamonds, on the other hand, are considered luxurious but are not necessary for life. The paradox is that the more essential good—water—has a much lower economic value. Price theory can explain this paradox through the principle of scarcity. Prices are set by the relationship between the demand for a good and its scarcity: water is valuable but not scarce, so it is priced lower than diamonds are.

In many ways, particularly in its belief that prices were self-regulating, the price theory of the Chicago school referred back to the "classical" tradition of economics that held sway before the critiques of Marx and Keynes.

Friedman's work also builds on the ideas of the economists Knut Wicksell* and Irving Fisher,* who were central to developing the idea of nominal* and real* interest rates. As Friedman writes: "Thanks to Wicksell we are all acquainted with the concept of a 'natural' rate of interest and the possibility of a discrepancy between the 'natural' and the 'market' rate."[10] To this, Fisher added the difference between real and nominal interest rates.[11]

Fisher stressed the importance of expectations about changes in prices, which Friedman later used as a key idea in "The Role": "Experience shows that the rate of interest will seldom adjust itself perfectly to changes in price level, because these changes are only in part foreseen."[12]

NOTES

1   Lionel Robbins, *An Essay on the Nature and Significance of Economic Science* (London: Macmillan, 1932), 15.

2   Adam Smith, *An Inquiry into the Nature and Causes of the Wealth of Nations: A Selected Edition* (Oxford: Oxford University Press, 1998).

3   Smith, *Wealth of Nations*, 62.

4   Smith, *Wealth of Nations*, 14.

5   Smith, *Wealth of Nations*, 14.

6   Karl Marx, *Capital: A Critique of Political Economy*, ed. Friedrich Engels (New York: Cosimo, 2007).

7   Marx, *Capital*, 708.

8   John Maynard Keynes, *General Theory of Employment, Interest, and Money*, accessed February 18, 2015, http://cas.umkc.edu/economics/people/facultypages/kregel/courses/econ645/winter2011/generaltheory.pdf.

9   Alan Blinder, "Keynesian Economics," Library of Economics and Liberty, accessed February 18, 2015, http://www.econlib.org/library/Enc/KeynesianEconomics.html.

10 Friedman, "The Role": 7.

11 Irving Fisher, *The Purchasing Power of Money* (New York: Cosimo, 2006).

12 Fisher, *Purchasing Power*, 210.

MODULE 3
THE PROBLEM

KEY POINTS

- Although Friedman wanted less government involvement in the economy, he favored a specific role for the national authorities: prudent management of the money supply* by the central bank.

- Friedman's paper was a response to five decades of work by the Federal Reserve* (America's central bank). During this time, two alternate approaches—monetary policy* (adjusting the money supply), and fiscal policy* (adjusting government spending)—fell in and out of favor as the best approach to improving economic performance.

- Friedman argued that governments had placed too much faith in the belief that by adjusting the amount of money available to the economy, it was possible to manage macroeconomic* indicators such as economic growth* and unemployment.*

Core Question

The "role" in the title of Milton Friedman's paper "The Role of Monetary Policy" refers to the part that monetary policy should play in broader economic management and policymaking.

"Monetary policy" refers to the government's regulation of the money supply—that is, either holding back the money in circulation, or printing more bills. Specifically, Friedman wanted to both "stress what monetary policy cannot do" and to "try to outline what it can do and how it can best make its contribution" to broader economic management.[1] He wanted to outline a vision for an effective

> ❝ There is wide agreement about the major goals of economic policy: high employment, stable prices, and rapid growth. There is less agreement that these goals are mutually compatible or, among those who regard them as incompatible .... [t]here is least agreement about the role that various instruments of policy can and should play in achieving the several goals. ❞
>
> Milton Friedman, "The Role of Monetary Policy"

monetary policy that would help achieve specific goals: namely, "high employment, stable prices and rapid growth."[2]

Alongside this goal, however, is Friedman's true intention: to challenge the economic consensus (that is, the most generally shared assumptions) of his time. Friedman saw monetary policy as just one area in which the government had too much control over the economy. He wanted less government involvement in the economy, and proposed a more limited monetary policy that would convince not only economists but policymakers, too. As he writes: "We are in danger of assigning to monetary policy a larger role than it can perform, in danger of asking it to accomplish, and, as a result, in danger of preventing it from making the contribution that it is capable of making."[3]

The Participants

Friedman's paper is a response to the five decades of monetary history that came before it. The Federal Reserve System*—America's central bank, also known as "the Fed"—was established in 1913 to regulate monetary policy in the United States. It was given the goals of "accommodating commerce and business" and looking after "the general credit situation of the economy."[4] Since the Fed was created, economists and policymakers have had changing views on exactly how effective it is.

During the early 1920s the Fed was praised for its "capacity for fine-tuning" the economy and was credited for the period's "relative stability."[5] Even after the financial crisis of 1929 and the Great Depression* that followed, many observers saw the Fed as crucial to recovery. In 1932, for example, the politician Adolph Sabath* said: "I insist it is within the power of the Federal Reserve Board to relieve the financial and commercial distress." He was referring to the sharp decrease in demand caused by the depression.*[6]

Until this point there had been a widespread belief that monetary policy—adjusting the money supply—could have a significant impact on things such as employment and growth. But this belief lost much of its appeal after John Maynard Keynes's* work was published in the 1930s. Keynes generally favored fiscal interventions (that is, government spending) over monetary actions. In 1934, for example, he wrote: "It is not easy to bring about business expansion merely by monetary manipulation. [Direct governmental spending], however, is infinitely more important and offers in my opinion much greater hopes."

In the 1950s, monetary policy regained a reputation as an important policy tool, largely due to the discovery of the Phillips Curve.* Named after the economist William Phillips,* the Phillips Curve shows a negative link between inflation* and unemployment: allowing more inflation, in other words, lowers unemployment, while clamping down on inflation leads to more unemployment.[7] Writing on this phenomenon, Phillips concluded: "The statistical evidence … seems in general to support the hypothesis … that the rate of change of money wage rates [one way of defining inflation] can be explained by the level of unemployment and the rate of change of unemployment."[8]

Though Phillips's discovery seemed to imply a strong relationship between inflation and unemployment, it was not until 1960 that economists in the United States came to view the Phillips Curve as an effective policy instrument.

That year, the economists Paul Samuelson* and Robert Solow* published a paper in which they estimated the Phillips Curve for the United States. Their conclusion was that an increase in prices of 4 to 5 percent per year "would seem to be the necessary cost of high employment and production in the years immediately ahead."[9]

Although Samuelson and Solow were skeptical of the reliability of the Phillips Curve in the long run, their paper was received as supporting the idea that the money supply could be used to achieve unemployment targets.[10] This is because allowing the money supply to grow brings more inflation, while limiting money supply holds down price rises.

The Contemporary Debate

It has been suggested that the Keynesian* position—widely followed when Friedman wrote "The Role of Monetary Policy"—was ripe for criticism. Referring to problems with the Phillips Curve, the economist Harry Johnson* wrote in 1970 that Keynes's approach had "suffered from the same major defect as the orthodoxy Keynes attacked—the attempt to explain essentially monetary phenomena in terms of a mixture of real theory and *ad-hoc*-ery" (by which he meant "making it up on the fly").[11] In that sense, "The Role" was well positioned. It was published at the right time, to an audience ready to receive its arguments.

Friedman was very well acquainted with both the history of monetary policy in the United States and shifting academic attitudes towards the role of money in the economy. His 1963 book *A Monetary History of the United States* included rich historical stories and paid a lot of attention to disputes about the direction of policy.[12] So his address to the American Economic Association, the inspiration for the paper, was delivered as a clear attack on the accepted ideas of the period.

Readers of the paper will be able to grasp this history without reading the original sources, as Friedman provides a summary. Still, some knowledge of the evolution of the accepted positions would be helpful for understanding Friedman's intentions. Friedman does not specifically call out his targets by name, referring only to "the views that prevail today."[13] Still, in the context of the speech, it is fair to assume that Friedman's audience were aware of his intended targets.

NOTES

1   Milton Friedman, "The Role of Monetary Policy," *American Economic Review* 58, no. 1 (March 1, 1968): 5.

2   Friedman, "The Role": 1.

3   Friedman, "The Role": 5.

4   "Federal Reserve Act of 1913," accessed February 18, 2015, http://legisworks.org/sal/38/stats/STATUTE-38–Pg251a.pdf.

5   Friedman, "The Role": 1.

6   Quoted in Milton Friedman and Anna J. Schwartz, *A Monetary History of the United States, 1867–1960* (Princeton, NJ: Princeton University Press, 1963), 409.

7   Alban Phillips, "The Relation between Unemployment and the Rate of Change of Money Wage Rates in the United Kingdom, 1861–1957," *Economica* 25, no. 100 (1958): 283–99.

8   Phillips, "Relation": 299.

9   Paul Samuelson and Robert Solow, "Analytical Aspects of Anti-Inflation Policy," *American Economic Review* 50, no. 2 (1960): 192.

10 Paul Krugman, "The Pigou Effect," accessed February 18, 2015, http://krugman.blogs.nytimes.com/2013/08/10/the-pigou-effect-double-super-special-wonkish/.

11 Harry Johnson, "The Keynesian Revolution and the Monetarist Counter-Revolution," *American Economic Review* 61, no. 2 (1971): 9.

12 Friedman and Schwartz, *A Monetary History*.

13 Friedman, "The Role": 5.

MODULE 4
THE AUTHOR'S CONTRIBUTION

KEY POINTS

- Friedman's prescription was simple: governments should drastically reduce their use of monetary policy* if they wanted to actively manage the economy. Instead, they should aim for a steady and predictable monetary policy.

- Friedman's contribution attacked decades of economic orthodoxy, which viewed markets—the labor market and the price of goods, for instance—as flawed and in need of strong and activist government intervention.

- Friedman's views were very similar to those of another economist, Edmund Phelps.* Neither of them agreed with the commonly held view that deliberately allowing higher inflation* brings lower unemployment,* and vice versa.

Author's Aims

In his paper "The Role of Monetary Policy," Milton Friedman argues that the interpretation of the Phillips Curve* associated with the economists Samuelson* and Solow* is wrong for two reasons. First, it fails to account for differences between nominal* and real* values. (Real values are adjusted for inflation. If your salary goes up by 2 percent in nominal terms, but inflation is 5 percent, then your *real* salary has gone down by 3 percent.) Second, it makes long-run predictions without taking into account people's *expectations* about the economy.

Friedman was not original in identifying these ideas; the Austrian American economist Gottfried Haberler,* for example, pointed to the role of expectations in 1960: "As creeping inflation continues,

❝ [It is] easily the most influential paper on macroeconomics ever published in the post-war era.**❞**
Robert Skidelsky, on "The Role of Monetary Policy"

more and more people will expect further rises in prices and will take steps to protect themselves … labor unions will ask for high wage increases in order to secure real improvement."[1] What was original about Friedman's argument was that it was clear, logical, and complete.

The paper unfolds over three parts.

First, Friedman provides a brief overview of how government and central bank policy has evolved since the beginning of the twentieth century, offering his own analysis of these policy shifts as he goes. This part of Friedman's paper is supported by his previous work on monetary economics, particularly his 1963 book *A Monetary History of the United States*, which he sometimes refers to merely as "recent studies."[2]

He then goes on to address his core aims. Here, he focuses on two areas in which monetary policy is, he believes, ineffective: setting exchange rates* between the currencies of different countries, and bringing down unemployment.

Lastly, he offers his own views for "how monetary policy should be conducted." A key part of Friedman's argument is his well-known belief in free enterprise and individual responsibility; he refers to these at the end of the paper, writing: "Steady monetary growth would provide a monetary climate favorable to the effective operation of those basic forces of enterprise, ingenuity, invention, hard work, and thrift that are the true springs of economic growth. This is the most that we can ask from monetary policy at our present stage of knowledge. But that much—and it is a great deal—is clearly within our reach."[3]

Approach

Like most of Friedman's academic work, in many ways "The Role" looks back to the "classical" economic tradition,* according to which an economy was something that regulated itself. Friedman saw the activist policymaking by governments—associated with John Maynard Keynes's* followers—as a betrayal of classical principles. He wanted to reintroduce classical ideas to economics by using a price-based approach.

Since World War II,* the Keynesian* school of thought had been the main approach to economic management in the academic and policy worlds, leading to Friedman's famous 1965 statement that "we are all Keynesians now."[4]

Friedman did not mean his statement to be entirely literal. As he explained, it was an embrace of Keynesian *methods* but not Keynesian *theory*: "We all use the Keynesian language and apparatus," he wrote, referring to Keynes's way of analyzing the economy using aggregate values (that is, the "grand totals" that indicate how an economy is performing).

Whatever he thought of Keynes's method of analysis, however, Friedman made it clear he did not accept the "initial Keynesian conclusions."[5] Specifically, Friedman rejected the idea that changes in the money supply—or any other governmental intervention—could change "natural" levels of unemployment in the marketplace. In this way, Friedman was informed by his embrace of price theory.*

According to price theory, it is the prices of goods and labor—rather than factors that government can control, like the size of the money supply—that should drive market behavior and the real economy.

Friedman's counter-position to Keynes is known as monetarism,* and is based on the following principles:

- long-run monetary neutrality (the principle that, in the long term, money supply *cannot* affect real variables such as unemployment)

- short-run monetary non-neutrality (the principle that, in the short term, changing the size of the money supply *can* bring about changes such as lowering unemployment)
- recognizing the difference between real* and nominal* interest rates
- using measures such as the overall money supply as the basis for analysis.[6]

One important part of the monetarist approach is the view that any kind of price controls (minimum wages, for example) will create market distortions. Monetarism also holds that monetary policy should focus on price stability and that it should be consistent over time.[7]

Contribution in Context

Although "The Role" was an original piece of work in many regards, many of Friedman's observations about monetary policy overlapped with observations about labor-market economics made that same year (1967) by the economist Edmund Phelps.*[8]

Both Friedman and Phelps argued there was no long-run trade-off between inflation and unemployment. In other words they did not agree with the idea—generally accepted by economists at the time and "proven" by the Phillips Curve—that deliberately allowing higher inflation brings lower unemployment, and vice versa. Phelps's paper is more model-based than Friedman's, but also builds on recognizing a difference between real and nominal wages and the idea of expectations. As Phelps writes, if the idea behind the Phillips Curve is accepted, "the expected rate of inflation must be added to it."[9] This is because "workers will only pay attention to real wages"; if they expect inflation to continue, they will demand higher wage increases to make up for inflation, in addition to any real increases in purchasing power.* So over time, expectations about costs and wages undermine the Phillips Curve's power to make correct predictions.[10]

A key factor common to both Phelps and Friedman is the idea of a natural rate of unemployment that cannot be changed in the long run by government actions such as pushing up inflation.

Friedman agreed that there were "enormous similarities and tremendous overlaps" between his work and Phelps's analysis. The main difference was that Friedman examined the issue from the angle of monetary policy and interest rates, while Phelps examined the issue from labor-market dynamics and wages. But, he agreed, his and Phelps's "theories are the same."[11]

NOTES

1   Quoted in James Forder, "The Historical Place of the 'Friedman–Phelps' Expectations Critique," Oxford Economics Discussion Paper Series 299 (July 2008), 6.

2   Milton Friedman, "The Role of Monetary Policy," *American Economic Review* 58, no. 1 (March 1, 1968): 3.

3   Friedman, "The Role": 17.

4   Milton Friedman, "The Economy: We Are All Keynesians Now", *Time*, December 31, 1965.

5   Quoted in Roger Garrison, "Hayek and Friedman: Head to Head," accessed February 18, 2015, http://www.auburn.edu/~garriro/hayek%20and%20friedman.pdf.

6   Bennett McCallum, "Monetarism," *Library of Economics and Liberty*, accessed February 18, 2015, http://www.econlib.org/library/Enc/Monetarism.html.

7   McCallum, "Monetarism."

8   Edmund Phelps, "Phillips Curves, Expectations of Inflation and Optimal Employment over Time," *Economica* 34, no. 135 (1967): 254–81.

9   Phelps, "Phillips Curves," 261.

10 Kevin Hoover, "Phillips Curve," accessed February 18, 2015, http://www.econlib.org/library/Enc/PhillipsCurve.html.

11 Quoted in Brian Snowdon and Howard R. Vane, *Modern Macroeconomics: Its Origins, Development and Current State* (Cheltenham: Edward Elgar, 2005), 205.

SECTION 2
IDEAS

MODULE 5
MAIN IDEAS

KEY POINTS

- In his paper, Friedman explores how theories of monetary policy* changed over time, the limits to the things that monetary policy can accomplish, and the theory that it should be conducted modestly.

- Friedman argues that governments expect too much from monetary policy. It cannot control inflation* or unemployment* in the long term, he says—and trying to use monetary policy in this way will eventually cause damage to economic growth.

- The paper is based on a speech Friedman wrote for an American Economic Association conference. He was presenting his ideas to fellow specialists, so assumes they understand the issues, and does not explain them for the non-specialist.

Key Themes

At the center of Milton Friedman's argument in "The Role of Monetary Policy" is the question of how a government can use monetary policy to manage the economy. It is a question that fits within the broader debate between Keynesian* and "classical"* economists, who have very different beliefs about the benefits of government intervention in a nation's economy. Friedman's analysis of this theme revolves around several economic indicators* including the money supply,* interest rates,* unemployment, and prices.

At the time he wrote the paper, policymakers mainly accepted the Keynesian view regarding monetary policy, which backed the

> **❝** I therefore shall, as my first task, stress what monetary policy cannot do. I shall then try to outline what it can do and how it can best make its contribution, in the present state of our knowledge—or ignorance. **❞**
>
> Milton Friedman, "The Role of Monetary Policy"

use of all mechanisms within a government's control in its attempts to manage the economy, stimulate demand, and keep unemployment low. Friedman sought to show that monetary policy was far less effective than Keynesian policymakers believed and might actually have harmful effects on economic stability.

There are several sub-themes underlying this core theme in Friedman's paper.

The first is the historical evolution of monetary policy and opinions on monetary policy from the 1920s to the late 1960s. In particular, Friedman is interested in the changing attitudes towards the idea that monetary policy can achieve specific outcomes in such things as inflation and unemployment.

In the 1920s, monetary policy was considered highly effective. It was widely held that "a new era had arrived in which business cycles* had been rendered obsolete by monetary technology"[1] (in other words, that management of the money supply would smooth out the economy's booms and busts). In the aftermath of the Great Depression,* however, "opinion swung to the other extreme," and monetary policy was seen as almost completely powerless in the face of economic crisis.[2] In the 1950s and 1960s, the dominant opinion changed again, and monetary policy was seen as a tool for managing economic outcomes. As Friedman, said: "Today, primacy [in monetary policy] is assigned to the promotion of full employment, with the prevention of inflation a continuing but definitely secondary concern."[3]

Friedman also explores the limits of monetary policy in his paper, and chooses to focus on two areas in which it is, he believes, ineffective: setting interest rates* and reducing unemployment "for more than very limited periods."[4] Interest rates and unemployment are central to the overall economy. So by showing them to be areas in which monetary policy has little effect, Friedman is making a strong statement.

Finally, Friedman discusses "how monetary policy should be conducted." He outlines his own preferences for what a central bank should do, inside certain limitations, to maintain a healthy economy.[5]

Friedman's core themes and sub-themes emerge in a logical and clear manner and lead to this idea: that the real goal of government policy should be promoting free enterprise, not managing indicators such as unemployment and inflation.

Exploring the Ideas

Friedman's main idea in "The Role" is that monetary policy is not an effective tool to achieve long-term inflation or unemployment targets, and instead, the goal of monetary policy should be to "avoid mistakes" and "provide a stable background to the economy."[6] Specifically, Friedman proposes that monetary policymakers should strive towards "adopting publicly the policy of achieving a steady rate of growth in a specified monetary total"—or in other words, gradually increasing the money supply in a constant and predictable way.[7]

Friedman's suggestion that governments should do no more than aim for steady increases in the quantity of money comes from his doubt that monetary policy can achieve more specific goals. He writes that "the first requirement is that the monetary authority should guide itself by magnitudes [outcomes] it can control, not by ones it cannot control."[8]

Further, he is motivated by his understanding of the causes of the Great Depression* (or "Great Contraction," as he calls it) and his belief that monetary authorities must avoid "sharp swings in policy."[9] As he writes: "In the past, monetary authorities have occasionally moved in the wrong direction—as in the episode of the Great Contraction."[10]

Here, he refers to the sudden decreases in the monetary supply in the immediate aftermath of the financial crisis of 1929. He goes on: "More frequently, they have moved in the right direction, albeit often too late, but have erred [made a mistake] by moving too far."[11]

According to Friedman, if monetary authorities maintained a "steady but moderate growth in the quantity of money," it would contribute to overall economic stability and would make a "major contribution to avoidance of either inflation or deflation* of prices."[12]

Language and Expression

As "The Role" was originally presented as a speech to an audience of economists, it is delivered in a direct and playful style, and assumes some knowledge of how monetary policy works. Friedman's tone is designed to appeal to specialists—and in particular to persuade fellow economists that their usual views are wrong. Friedman frequently uses the pronoun "you" to describe his audience, a stylistic choice unusual for academic papers and one that makes this paper seem more like an informal seminar presentation than an academic work.

Readers will be more comfortable with the paper if they acquaint themselves with the jargon and core ideas of macroeconomics* such as unemployment, interest rates, and exchange rates.* Further, readers should come to the paper with some general knowledge of what monetary policy is—Friedman does not provide definitions or context.

Unlike many economics papers, "The Role" does not use mathematics. But it does, however, rely on tight verbal arguments that readers may struggle with if they are unfamiliar with the ideas.

Understanding the difference between nominal* and real* values is central to his argument, for example. But when he discusses this difference, he does so without providing the reader with any summary of what those terms mean.[13]

NOTES

1   Milton Friedman, "The Role of Monetary Policy," *American Economic Review* 58, no. 1 (March 1, 1968): 1.

2   Friedman, "The Role": 1.

3   Friedman, "The Role": 5.

4   Friedman, "The Role": 5.

5   Friedman, "The Role": 14.

6   Friedman, "The Role": 12–13

7   Friedman, "The Role": 16.

8   Friedman, "The Role": 14.

9   Friedman, "The Role": 15.

10 Friedman, "The Role": 15.

11 Friedman, "The Role": 16.

12 Friedman, "The Role": 17.

13 Friedman, "The Role": 8.

MODULE 6
SECONDARY IDEAS

KEY POINTS

- The secondary ideas in Friedman's article include an explanation of the weakness of the Phillips Curve:* the fact that it ignores the distinction between nominal* and real* wages. He also examines the "natural rate of unemployment"*—a rate that monetary policy* could not affect in the long term.

- The article gives examples to show the mechanism by which a decision to increase the money supply* would initially fuel economic activity, before the old equilibrium soon re-established itself.

- More attention has been paid to Friedman's views on unemployment in the paper than on interest rates.*

Other Ideas

The most important secondary idea in Milton Friedman's "The Role of Monetary Policy" is his critique of the Phillips Curve—a critique which supports his attack on overly ambitious monetary policy in general.

Friedman's argument centers on the difference between real and nominal wages. Nominal wages are simply the price tag for a good or service. So a worker in 1960 earning seven dollars per hour would have a nominal wage of seven dollars per hour. Real wages, on the other hand, are adjusted for changes in the price level over time. Since price levels* tend to rise due to inflation,* a seven-dollar wage in 1960 would be worth more than a seven-dollar wage a worker earned today, even though the nominal wages are identical.

> ❝ I fear that, now … the pendulum may well have swung too far, that, now … we are in danger of assigning to monetary policy a larger role than it can perform, in danger of asking it to accomplish tasks that it cannot achieve, and, as a result, in danger of preventing it from making the contribution that it is capable of making. ❞
>
> Milton Friedman, "The Role of Monetary Policy"

In other words, we are adjusting for *purchasing power,** which is the amount of goods and services a specific nominal value can buy in a given period. Seven dollars could buy a lot more in 1960 than it can today, so the *real* wage of that worker expressed in 2015 terms would be much higher than seven dollars.

Another important idea in the paper is the "natural rate of unemployment"—in other words, the unemployment rate that would hold when the economy is well balanced.[1] Crucially, for Friedman, the natural rate of unemployment is unaffected by monetary factors—it is related almost exclusively to structural features of the economy such as whether raw materials are available at reasonable prices, or whether there are enough people educated and trained to do all the jobs in the economy. Friedman notes that the natural rate is not fixed, and in fact will change as the structure of the economy changes. For example, Friedman argues that "legal minimum wage rates" and "the strength of labor unions" will have a tendency to increase the natural rate of unemployment by making it more expensive for firms to make new hires.[2] By contrast, "improvements in employment exchanges" and "availability of information about job vacancies and labor supply" will tend to lower the natural rate.[3]

Exploring the Ideas

Friedman praises the Phillips Curve as an "important and original contribution" to economic thought, but challenges its basic defect: its "failure to distinguish between *nominal* and *real* wages."[4] Whereas the Phillips Curve suggests policymakers can target unemployment rates by increasing or decreasing inflation through adjustments of the money supply, Friedman shows that the impact only holds in the short run. Over time, *expectations* about inflation will undo the unemployment targets established in the short run.

To show why, Friedman provides an example. First, assume the monetary authority attempts to set unemployment at 3 percent, which is also assumed to be below the natural rate.[5] Further, assume the economy has most recently gone through a period of stable prices (that is, low inflation) and stubborn unemployment of higher than 3 percent. In order to achieve lower unemployment, the monetary authority "increases the rate of monetary growth."[6] The infusion of cash into the economy will increase spending as lower borrowing costs stimulate business to expand operations, and since one person's spending is another person's income, both spending and income will rise in the economy.

As Friedman notes, the initial effects of this increase will be felt in production and employment rather than in prices: "Producers will tend to react to the initial expansion in … demand by increasing output, employees by working longer hours, and the unemployed by taking jobs that open up as firms hire more workers to meet the increased demand."[7] Thus, in the short run, the policy has had its desired effect: the infusion of money into the economy increased output and lowered the unemployment rate.

According to Friedman, however, these are only the "initial effects."[8] Over time, the prices that goods sell at will increase in response to the new demand created by the monetary expansion. And this will lower real wages which are, of course, nominal wages adjusted for prices.

Wages tend to increase more slowly than prices, so as the price of goods and services rises, workers' purchasing power will fall. And as workers see their real wages fall, they will demand higher nominal wages. Eventually unemployment will move back to the natural rate as employers cut back the number of people they hire at the new, higher wages. In order for the monetary authority to achieve its target of 3 percent unemployment, it would have to increase the money supply further, which would raise inflation.

According to Friedman, the only way the monetary authority can maintain its target rate of unemployment is with "accelerating inflation"—that is, by constantly increasing it.

Friedman makes a very similar argument for interest rates, showing that monetary policy can do little to maintain interest rate targets in the long run.[9]

Overlooked

Friedman's paper was first delivered as an address to the American Economic Association, the country's foremost professional organization for economists, and later published in the *American Economic Review*, one of the most important economics journals. Given all this initial attention, and the continued attention the paper has received in the decades since its publication, there is little in it that has been overlooked. What is more, it is also a very short work at only 17 pages in length, meaning most informed commentators have thoroughly examined all the ideas Friedman expresses in it.

Since the article's publication in 1968, leading figures in modern macroeconomics,* from the Nobel Prize*-winning economist Paul Krugman* to the economist John Cochrane,* have analyzed it and picked it apart.[10] Interest in different areas of the text has grown and fallen over the years, but Friedman's critique of the Phillips Curve and his support for a steady monetary policy have remained front and center in the discussion.

The one area of the paper that has received relatively less attention is Friedman's discussion of interest rates. Like his critical discussion of the Phillips Curve, Friedman did not think that monetary policy could set interest rates "for more than very limited periods."[11] It is likely that this has received less attention because much of the policy discussion, both when the paper came out and in the debate that followed its publication, focused on employment rather than on interest rates.

NOTES

1   Milton Friedman, "The Role of Monetary Policy," *American Economic Review* 58, no. 1 (March 1, 1968): 7–8.

2   Friedman, "The Role": 9.

3   Friedman, "The Role": 9.

4   Friedman, "The Role": 8.

5   Friedman, "The Role": 9–10.

6   Friedman, "The Role": 9.

7   Friedman, "The Role": 10.

8   Friedman, "The Role": 10.

9   Friedman, "The Role": 5–6.

10 Paul Krugman, "Who Was Milton Friedman?", accessed February 18, 2015, http://www.nybooks.com/articles/archives/2007/feb/15/who-was-milton-friedman/; and John Cochrane, "The Role of Monetary Policy Revisited," accessed February 18, 2015, http://bfi.uchicago.edu/feature-story/role-monetary-policy-revisited.

11 Friedman, "The Role": 5.

MODULE 7
ACHIEVEMENT

KEY POINTS

- Friedman's article had a big impact. Even leading left-wing* critics agreed that Friedman succeeded in pointing out key weaknesses of the Keynesian* approach, especially by showing that the supposed trade-off between inflation* and unemployment* was only temporary.

- Yet when Friedman's approach to economics, known as monetarism,* was followed by right-wing governments in the US and the UK in the 1980s, the results were mixed.

- Although Friedman remains popular with libertarians,* for others his legacy has been harmed by his association with right-wing figures such as Chile's dictator Augusto Pinochet.* But even his critics think he is a great economist.

Assessing the Argument

Milton Friedman was hugely successful in achieving his aims. His paper "The Role of Monetary Policy" had an immediate influence on the economics profession, even on people who criticized him such as the Keynesian economist James Tobin.* As the Nobel Prize-winning economist Paul Krugman* writes: "Friedman's critique of Keynes became so influential largely because he correctly identified Keynesianism's weak points."[1]

The Swedish economist Erik Lundberg* presented Friedman with the 1976 Nobel Prize in Economics* by saying: "Friedman was the first to show that the prevalent assumption of a simple 'trade-off' between unemployment and the rate of inflation only held temporarily as a transient phenomenon."[2] Friedman's critique also had

> **❝** [It is] very likely the most influential article ever
> published in an economics journal. **❞**
>
> James Tobin, economist and frequent critic of Friedman

a political impact. For example, several chairmen of the US Federal
Reserve* Bank were forced to defend their activist policies in the face
of Friedman's criticisms. In 1969, Friedman even called for Federal
Reserve Chairman William McChesney Martin Jr.* to resign.[3]

The British economists Brian Snowdon and Howard Vane write:
"While *A Monetary History* has undoubtedly been Friedman's most
influential book ... 'The Role of Monetary Policy' has certainly
been his most influential article." In 1994, Krugman argued that
Friedman's article was "one of the decisive achievements of the post-
war era," while Robert Skidelsky* wrote in 1996 that it was "easily
the most influential paper on macroeconomics ever published in the
post-war era."[4] "The Role of Monetary Policy" remains one of the
most heavily quoted papers in economics. Monetarism, meanwhile,
went on to strongly influence policy choices in the United States
and the United Kingdom during the 1980s as both countries sought
to tame inflation. In the UK this was referred to as "[Prime Minister
Margaret] Thatcher's* Monetarist Experiment."[5]

Achievement in Context

"The Role" has had a deep impact on public policy around the globe.

In 2004, before becoming chairman of the US Federal Reserve,
and thereby the most powerful monetary policymaker in the world,
Ben Bernanke* noted in a famous speech: "For much of the late
1960s and the 1970s ... many economists and policymakers held
the view that policy could exploit a permanent trade-off between
inflation and unemployment, as described by a simple Phillips
Curve* relationship. The idea of a permanent trade-off opened

up the beguiling possibility that, in return for accepting just a bit more inflation, policymakers could deliver a permanently low rate of unemployment. This view is now discredited, of course, on both theoretical and empirical grounds."

Bernanke pointed to Friedman's 1968 article as having "provided a major theoretical critique of the idea of a permanent trade-off," although he pointed out that "scholars disagree about when and to what degree US monetary policymakers absorbed the lessons of Friedman's article."[6]

The results of Friedman's ideas being put into action have been mixed. The experiments with monetarism in the United Kingdom and the United States during the 1980s are widely believed by those on the left of the political divide to have caused mass unemployment and the weakening of the welfare state, particularly in the UK. Significantly, Friedman went on to serve as an unofficial advisor to US President Ronald Reagan* during the presidential campaign of 1980. Despite the widespread adoption of his ideas in the fields of economics and public policy, the ideas Friedman discusses in his article have found limited application in broader fields of study.

Limitations

Reactions to Friedman's work often are often tied up with how one feels about his libertarian* political views. In particular, those on the left strongly oppose his belief in minimal state interference in the economy. Human rights advocates, meanwhile, have been highly critical of his promotion of free-market* ideas abroad, particularly his consultations with the notorious Pinochet regime in Chile in the mid-1970s, where Friedman suggested reducing government spending to reduce inflation.[7] Indeed, left-wing protestors interrupted his Nobel Prize ceremony in 1976 on humanitarian grounds.

Recently, the Canadian author Naomi Klein* strongly criticized Friedman in her book *The Shock Doctrine*. In reference to Friedman's support for private education, Klein writes: "For more than three decades, Friedman and his powerful followers had been perfecting this very strategy: waiting for a major crisis, then selling off pieces of the state to private players while citizens were still reeling from the shock."[8]

Those on the libertarian end of the political spectrum, meanwhile, tend to view Friedman's work as a recipe for a more efficient and free society—though they often refer to Friedman's other papers, not "The Role." Academic economists, on the other hand, tend to judge his work on its intellectual merits. Krugman, for example, a prominent critic of Friedman, admits that he was a "great economist and a great man."[9] Depending on one's political and professional background, then, it is possible to interpret Friedman's work in various ways.

NOTES

1   Paul Krugman, "Who Was Milton Friedman?" accessed February 18, 2015, http://www.nybooks.com/articles/archives/2007/feb/15/who-was-milton-friedman/.

2   Quoted in James Forder, "The Historical Place of the 'Friedman–Phelps' Expectations Critique," Oxford Economics Discussion Paper Series 299 (July 2008), 2.

3   Edward Nelson, "Milton Friedman and US Monetary History: 1961–2006," Federal Reserve Bank of St. Louis, Working Paper Series (2007), accessed February 18, 2015, http://research.stlouisfed.org/wp/2007/2007-002.pdf.

4   Quoted in Brian Snowdon and Howard R. Vane, *Modern Macroeconomics: Its Origins, Development and Current State* (Cheltenham: Edward Elgar, 2005), 175.

5   Snowdon and Vane, *Modern Macroeconomics*, 175.

6   Ben Bernanke, "The Great Moderation," presented at the Eastern Economic Association, Washington, DC, February 20, 2004, accessed July 25, 2013, http://www.federalreserve.gov/BOARDDOCS/SPEECHES/2004/20040220/default.htm.

7   Naomi Klein, *The Shock Doctrine: The Rise of Disaster Capitalism* (Toronto: Knopf Canada, 2009).

8   Klein, *The Shock Doctrine*, accessed February 18, 2015, http://www.naomiklein.org/shock-doctrine/excerpt.

9   Krugman, "Who Was Milton Friedman?"

MODULE 8
PLACE IN THE AUTHOR'S WORK

KEY POINTS

- Friedman made important contributions to different fields of economics, including consumer choice* and the history of monetary policy,* in most cases attacking then widely accepted Keynesian* ideas.

- Friedman was a public intellectual who fought openly for governments to adopt free-market* policies.

- "The Role of Monetary Policy" represents one of the author's most important contributions to global monetary policymaking. It was part of a broader body of work that won him the Nobel Prize in Economics* in 1976.

Positioning

"The Role of Monetary Policy" was written at the height of Milton Friedman's academic powers in 1967. Earlier, he had written papers on a variety of subjects in economics, including consumer choice, economic methodology, and monetary history. He worked on many areas of economics in his career, but his ideological orientation in favor of free markets and free enterprise always came through.

One of Friedman's famous early works is the 1957 book *A Theory of the Consumption Function*. In it, he introduced the permanent income hypothesis:* the idea that consumption* (that is, spending on goods and services) in any period is related both to a person's *present* income and their expected *future* income.[1]

This hypothesis was a direct challenge to Keynes's argument that "individuals and households adjust their expenditures on consumption to reflect their current income."[2] In other words,

> **❝** The Great Depression, like most other periods of severe unemployment, was produced by government mismanagement rather than by any inherent instability of the private economy. **❞**
>
> Milton Friedman, *Capitalism and Freedom*

Keynes proposed that an individual's monthly spending habits should only depend on their income in a given month—and therefore if they earn more in any month, they will change their spending and saving patterns. Friedman's model, however, took account of "consumption, wealth, and income"[3] to show that a person's current consumption should be explained by their expectations about their wealth and earnings in the long term. This is just one example of Friedman's strong challenges to Keynesianism.

Friedman's book *A Monetary History* (1963), co-authored with the economist Anna Schwartz,* largely paved the way for "The Role of Monetary Policy." The book marked a basic shift in the understanding of the causes of the Great Depression* (or "Great Contraction," as Friedman referred to it) and changed the course of monetary policy by forcing policymakers to see the importance of money in the overall dynamics of the economy.[4]

Referring to the sharp decline in the money stock (the total amount of money in circulation) that occurred as the economy of the United States contracted, Friedman writes: "It is hardly conceivable that money income could have declined by over one-half and prices by over one-third in the course of four years if there had been no decline in the stock of money."[5]

Before the publication of *A Monetary History*, the leading view—again, a position connected to John Maynard Keynes's* *General Theory*—was that monetary policy had little impact on the economy during a crisis. But Friedman's book tracks monetary policy over nearly a century in the United States to support the argument that the Federal Reserve's* decision to limit the amount of money in circulation contributed greatly to the Great Depression.

In addition to his technical work in economics, Friedman was highly visible as a public intellectual. He spoke regularly on public policy topics, including education, drug policy, and foreign policy, nearly always proposing a free-market position. He was also known for his work advising foreign governments, often on monetary issues. In a 1975 letter to the Chilean President Augusto Pinochet,* for example, Friedman suggested he reduce "drastically the rate of increase in the quantity of money" in order to avoid rapid inflation and harm to the economy.[6]

Integration

Friedman has rightly earned the reputation as one of the greatest economic thinkers of all time. The *Economist* magazine has described him as "the most influential economist of the second half of the twentieth century ... possibly of all of it."[7] Ben Bernanke,* who went on to serve as chairman of the US Federal Reserve, described him in the following terms: "Among economic scholars, Friedman has no peer. His seminal contributions to economics are legion, including his development of the permanent-income theory of consumer spending, his paradigm-shifting research in monetary economics, and his stimulating and original essays on economic history and methodology."[8]

With such a towering career, it is difficult to judge Friedman's influence on just one dimension, particularly as his work stretched across many areas of economics and politics. Still, a few themes are found throughout his work.

First, as noted above, many of Friedman's works were produced as attacks on what he called "naïve Keynesianism," which was the dominant economic point of view prior to the 1970s.[9] In that sense,

Friedman was an ideologue*—he tended to disagree with Keynes and fought for the view that government should have a limited role in the economy. Within this context, Friedman's work on monetary policy should be seen as just one part of a larger mission to shift economic thinking and policy towards free-market principles.

Significance

Friedman body of work is immense and highly influential. His Nobel Prize in Economics, awarded in 1976, was given "for his achievements in the fields of consumption analysis, monetary history and theory and for his demonstration of the complexity of [economic] stabilization policy."[10] His work on monetary economics is significant to his career, in other words, but it is still only a portion of his work.

In some ways, the continuing significance of "The Role" is tied to the evolution of monetarism* in economic thought. Monetarism's popularity grew in the 1960s, and was given a strong push when Friedman's paper was published in 1968. But its popularity declined in the 1970s and 1980s, according to the economist Bennett McCallum,* as the monetarist idea that money demand was constant gave way to the idea that, in fact, the demand for money "shifted significantly and unpredictably from quarter to quarter."[11] Friedman's support for a constant rate of money growth does not seem workable in a world in which the demand for money goes up and down regularly.

The decline of monetarism is rooted in real world events, too. Between 1979 and 1982, the Federal Reserve attempted a "monetarist experiment" to reduce high inflation rates that had continued during the 1970s and attempted to "hit specified monthly targets for the growth rate" of the money supply.[12] The experiment limited the money supply, which had the effect of increasing short-term interest rates and reducing business activity. The result was the "deepest recession since the Great Depression of the 1930s."[13] This experiment is seen today as having been a necessary "attack on inflation," but observers at the time viewed it as a "macroeconomic* disaster."[14]

While Friedman's suggestion of a steady monetary policy is somewhat out of favor today, the seeds of his ideas, particularly the critique of the Phillips Curve,* remain important.

NOTES

1 Milton Friedman, *A Theory of the Consumption Function* (Princeton, NJ: Princeton University Press: 1957).

2 "Milton Friedman," Library of Economics and Liberty, accessed February 18, 2015, http://www.econlib.org/library/Enc/bios/Friedman.html.

3 Friedman, *Consumption*, 6.

4 Milton Friedman and Anna J. Schwartz, *A Monetary History of the United States, 1867–1960* (Princeton, NJ: Princeton University Press, 1963).

5 Friedman and Schwartz, *A Monetary History*, 301.

6 Milton Friedman, "Letter to General Pinochet on Our Return from Chile and His Reply," accessed February 18, 2015, http://wwww.naomiklein.org/files/resources/pdfs/friedman-pinochet-letters.pdf last.

7 "Milton Friedman, a Giant among Economists," *The Economist*, November 23, 2006.

8 Bernanke, "On Milton Friedman's Ninetieth Birthday," accessed February 18, 2015, http://www.federalreserve.gov/boarddocs/Speeches/2002/20021108/default.htm.

9 "Interview with Milton Friedman," Public Broadcasting Service, accessed February 18, 2015, http://www.pbs.org/wgbh/commandingmheights/shared/minitext/int_miltonfriedman.html#7.

10 "Milton Friedman—Facts," Nobelprize.org, accessed February 18, 2015, http://www.nobelprize.org/nobel_prizes/economic-sciences/laureates/1976/friedman-facts.html.

11 Bennett McCallum, "Monetarism," Library of Economics and Liberty, accessed February 18, 2015, http://www.econlib.org/library/Enc/Monetarism.html.

12 McCallum, "Monetarism."

13 McCallum, "Monetarism."

14 McCallum, "Monetarism."

SECTION 3
IMPACT

MODULE 9
THE FIRST RESPONSES

KEY POINTS

- Critical responses to Friedman's paper came mainly from Keynesian* economists. Above all, they attacked Friedman's claim that it was pointless for a government to try to lower the unemployment* rate below what Friedman called its "natural" level.

- In the 1970s, the existence of "stagflation"* (a word acknowledging the stagnation and inflation* affecting certain Western economies) seemed to support Friedman's rejection of the claim—supported by the Phillips Curve*— that you could achieve low unemployment if you were prepared to tolerate high inflation.

- Friedman's call for a steady growth rate for the money supply* is seen today as ineffective. But the monetarism* that he championed has had a big impact, especially the idea that careful monetary policy* can be effective in stabilizing the economy.

Criticism

Much of the critical debate around Milton Friedman's ideas focused on his monetarist views in general, and not the specific argument in "The Role of Monetary Policy." Still, some critics in the Keynesian tradition responded directly to the paper.

One of his most prominent Keynesian critics was James Tobin.* In Tobin's address to the American Economic Association in 1971, he challenged Friedman's understanding of the "natural rate" of unemployment, which is at the heart of the analysis in "The Role."

" Now I am a *Keynesian.* **"**
US President Richard Nixon, 1971

Friedman believed that the natural rate resulted from structural features such as the development of the economy, the education of the workforce, and so on. Tobin questioned the validity of the concept. For him, government action should be able to reduce levels of unemployment below any "natural" rate: "Friedman advised the monetary authorities not to seek to improve upon [the natural rate of unemployment]. But in fact we know little about the existence of [any state of balance] that allows for all the imperfections and frictions that explain why the natural rate is bigger than zero."[1]

In contrast to Friedman's view—that there is an amount of unemployment that a government will simply have to live with, since there is a maximum number of people any economy can employ—Tobin argued the natural rate could be reduced with appropriate government policies.[2]

Friedman was also the target of criticisms from monetarists. Karl Brunner* and Allan Meltzer,* for example, writing in reference to Friedman's ideas on monetary policy in general and not just those in "The Role," saw Friedman's theories as not "a particularly useful basis for [experimental] work."[3] Brunner and Meltzer saw Friedman's theory as too vague, and criticized it for not incorporating experimental findings such as the "variability of the lag of monetary policy"[4] (that is, how long it takes for changes in monetary policy to have an effect on the economy).

Responses

Friedman remained firm in his challenge of the Phillips Curve* throughout his career. As a public statement in support of the monetarist position, he dedicated much of his 1976 Nobel Prize* acceptance speech to the topic. In that lecture, he pointed out that he was challenging a view held by most economists: "The 'natural-rate' or 'accelerationist' or 'expectations-adjusted' Phillips Curve hypothesis—as it has been variously designated—is by now widely accepted by economists, though by no means universally."[5]

He then offered a summary, over three steps, of how thinking about the Phillips Curve had changed. His brief history began with the observation of New Zealand ecomonist William Phillips* that inflation and unemployment are inversely linked. The second step was the argument, made independently by Friedman and the economist Edmund Phelps,* that the link between inflation and unemployment was not as simple as Phillips had claimed. The third and final step was what Friedman considered to be the emergence of an upside-down Phillips Curve: "In recent years, higher inflation has often been accompanied by higher not lower unemployment, especially for several years in length."[6] This stagflation—the combination of stagnation and high unemployment with price inflation that plagued the United States and Britain in the 1970s—was seen to support Friedman's critique.

As for his monetarist critics, Friedman accepted their criticisms, noting: "I largely agree with Brunner and Meltzer, who do not comment in any detail on my interpretation of Keynes.* The appearance of disagreement simply reflects their gracious assumption that my objective was more ambitious than it was."[7] In a sign of friendship, Friedman also cited Brunner and Meltzer in his Nobel Prize address, though he did not mention Tobin or any other Keynesian economists directly.

Conflict and Consensus

Friedman's proposal for a constant growth-rate monetary rule—that is, that the rate of monetary growth should correspond to the approximate long-term growth rate of the economy—has fallen out of favor among policymakers. But monetarism has nevertheless made an enormous and lasting contribution to macroeconomics* and current policymaking. The American economist Bennett McCallum* notes that "most research economists today accept, at least tacitly, the proposition that monetary policy is more useful than fiscal policy* for stabilizing the economy."[8] Furthermore, monetary authorities have largely absorbed Friedman's assertions regarding what monetary policy can and cannot do.

As Kevin Hoover,* an economist whose research focus has included the history of twentieth-century macroeconomics, writes: "The 1970s provided striking confirmation of Friedman and Phelps' fundamental point. Contrary to the original Phillips Curve, when the average inflation rate rose from about 2.5 percent in the 1960s to about 7 percent in the 1970s, the unemployment rate not only did not fall, it actually rose from about 4 percent to above 6 percent."[9] This kind of reversal in the Phillips Curve seemed to challenge Tobin's idea that government interventions in the market can drive unemployment closer to zero.

In addition, as Brian Snowdon and Howard Vane describe it, "perhaps the most important and lasting contribution of monetarism has been to persuade many economists to accept the idea that the potential of activist *discretionary* fiscal and monetary policy is much more limited than conceived prior to the monetarist counter-revolution."[10]

In other words, the experience of recent decades has had a sobering effect on policymakers. Those who believed in the power of governmental economic policymaking before Friedman's paper found out that it is less effective than it seemed to be. In that sense, Friedman won the debate with Keynesianism.

NOTES

1   James Tobin, "Inflation and Unemployment," *American Economic Review* 62, no. 1 (1972): 6.

2   Tobin, "Inflation and Unemployment": 15.

3   Karl Brunner and Allan Meltzer, "Friedman's Monetary Theory," *Journal of Political Economy* 80, no. 5 (1972): 837.

4   Brunner and Meltzer, "Friedman's Monetary Theory," 849.

5   Milton Friedman, "Inflation and Unemployment," Nobel Memorial Lecture, December 13, 1976, accessed February 18, 2015, http://www.nobelprize.org/nobel_prizes/economic-sciences/laureates/1976/friedman-lecture.pdf.

6   Friedman, "Inflation and Unemployment."

7   Milton Friedman, "Comments on the Critics," *Journal of Political Economy* 80 (1972): 907.

8   Bennett McCallum, "Monetarism," Library of Economics and Liberty, accessed February 18, 2015, http://www.econlib.org/library/Enc/Monetarism.html.

9   Kevin Hoover, "Phillips Curve," Library of Economics and Liberty, accessed February 18, 2015, http://www.econlib.org/library/Enc/PhillipsCurve.html.

10 Quoted in Brian Snowdon and Howard R. Vane, *Modern Macroeconomics: Its Origins, Development and Current State* (Cheltenham: Edward Elgar, 2005), 197.

MODULE 10
THE EVOLVING DEBATE

KEY POINTS

- Friedman's work paved the way for important developments in macroeconomics,* including the "rational expectations"* approach, which assumes that people and firms make rational and accurate predictions about things such as inflation.*

- The monetarist* school of economics grew out of Friedman's work. Although it has continued evolving, it is often associated with Friedman's proposal for a steady growth of the money supply*—a proposal that has fallen almost completely out of favor.

- In recent decades, there has been a blending of the monetarist and Keynesian* approaches. Followers are usually referred to as "New Keynesians."*

Uses and Problems

Milton Friedman's "The Role of Monetary Policy" and his other work inspired developments in macroeconomics for several decades. One of the key approaches that emerged out of the paper was the "rational expectations" economics associated with economists such as Robert Lucas* and Thomas Sargent.*

Lucas's paper "Expectations and the Neutrality of Money" (1972) took Friedman's analysis of the Phillips Curve* as its starting point and developed a model in which "all prices are market clearing, all agents behave optimally in light of their objectives and expectations, and expectations are formed optimally"—in other words, people and firms are able to behave perfectly rationally in the economy.[1]

> ❝ The influence of monetarism on how we all think about macroeconomics today has been deep, pervasive, and subtle. ❞
>
> Bradford J. Delong, "The Triumph of Monetarism?"

These assumptions are directly related to Friedman's critique of the Phillips Curve in the following way. Friedman showed that the only reason a rise in inflation causes even a short-term increase in employment is that workers do not immediately notice that prices are going up and their wages are losing purchasing power.* In other words, *real* wages are falling, giving employers an incentive to hire more workers. But soon workers pay attention to the inflation and expect that prices will continue to rise. Based on their rational expectations, they in turn demand greater wage increases to bring their *real* wages back up to their former level. At this point, inflation stops bringing higher employment rates.* As Thomas Sargent writes, "rational expectations undermines the idea that policymakers can manipulate the economy by systematically making the public have false expectations."[2]

Schools of Thought

The monetarist school with which "The Role" is associated has evolved and developed since the mid-1960s. In many ways, the school has been connected to what was seen as the failure of Friedman's proposal for a steadily increasing money supply. As the economist Willem Buiter* noted in 2003: "Friedman's prescription of a constant growth rate for some monetary aggregate* [a stock of money] is completely out of favor today … and has been for at least a couple of decades."[3] Although most monetary authorities now subscribe to Friedman's central idea of providing a stable monetary background, virtually none supports a fixed rate of money growth.

In other words, Friedman's views about the *role* of monetary policy have been accepted by policymakers and the economics discipline, but his views about the way it should be formulated and carried out have not. As the monetary economist Bennett McCallum notes: "Friedman's constant money growth rule, rather than other equally fundamental aspects of monetarism, attracted the most attention, thereby detracting from the understanding and appreciation of monetarism."[4]

McCallum goes on to argue that the key features of monetarism today came out of Friedman's critique of the Phillips Curve. The primary parts of the monetarist critique to Keynesianism that continue to be viewed as valid today are the distinction between real* and nominal* variables, and the rejection of a "long-run trade-off between inflation and unemployment."*[5]

In Current Scholarship

There is some irony in the fact that in today's economic debates most experts in the monetarist tradition would likely identify themselves as "New Keynesians" due to the blending of monetarist and Keynesian ideas that occurred in the 1980s and 1990s. According to Gregory Mankiw,* one of the most prominent specialists in the New Keynesian tradition, the term refers to economists who responded to the new classical* school of monetarism with "adjustments to the original Keynesian [principles]."[6]

According to Bradford Delong,* an economist most associated with the left of the political spectrum, there are five parts to the New Keynesian approach. Some of these parts come directly from Friedman's monetarism.

First, New Keynesians believe that frictions in the economy—burdensome regulations, for example, or a lack of information on the part of buyers and sellers, among other potential barriers—are the primary cause of economic fluctuations (booms and busts) known as business cycles.*

Second, they believe that "monetary policy is a more potent and useful tool for stabilization than is fiscal policy."

Third, that business cycles are best analyzed as departures from "the sustainable long-run trend."

Fourth, the best way to practice macroeconomic policy is to apply a "rule" rather than to analyze each episode "in isolation."

Fifth, that any approach to stabilization must "recognize the limits of stabilization policy."[7]

The similarities to Friedman's work are clear; his challenge of the Phillips Curve was a reminder of the limitations of policies meant to stabilize the economy. Moreover, Friedman always argued for the relative importance of monetary over fiscal policy. Further, following a general policy rule can be seen as similar to Friedman's proposal of a steady increase in the money supply. As Delong notes: "All five planks of the New Keynesian research program listed above had much of their development inside the twentieth century monetarist tradition, and all are associated with the name of Milton Friedman."[8]

NOTES

1   Robert Lucas, "Expectations and the Neutrality of Money," *Journal of Economic Theory* 4 (1972): 103.

2   Thomas Sargent, "Rational Expectations," http://www.econlib.org/library/Enc/RationalExpectations.html last accessed February 18, 2015.

3   Quoted in Brian Snowdon and Howard R. Vane, *Modern Macroeconomics: Its Origins, Development and Current State* (Cheltenham: Edward Elgar, 2005), 196.

4   Bennett McCallum, "Monetarism," Library of Economics and Liberty, accessed February 18, 2015, http://www.econlib.org/library/Enc/Monetarism.html.

5   McCallum, "Monetarism."

6   Gregory Mankiw, "New Keynesian Economics," Library of Economics and Liberty, accessed February 18, 2015, http://www.econlib.org/library/Enc/NewKeynesianEconomics.html.

7   Bradford Delong, "The Triumph of Monetarism?" *Journal of Economic Perspectives* 14, no. 1 (2000): 83–4.

8   Delong, "Triumph": 84.

IMPACT AND INFLUENCE TODAY

KEY POINTS

- Friedman's paper is still very relevant. Many of its proposals of what monetary authorities should and should not do have been widely accepted.

- Friedman played a broad public role as a top economist, a pioneer of monetarism,* and a cheerleader for free-market* capitalism.*

- The debate remains largely polarized between those who argue for increased government intervention in the economy and those, like Friedman, arguing for less.

Position

Milton Friedman's paper "The Role of Monetary Policy" is still very much a part of the current intellectual debate. Many of its lessons about the "proper" role for a successful monetary authority have been accepted, broadly speaking. But the question of how to conduct monetary policy* itself remains the subject of a highly important and evolving academic and policy debate. It is a question that concerns the entire discipline of economics.

As Friedman highlights in his paper, imagining the economy as a series of interconnected machines, "when [monetary policy] gets out of order, it throws a monkey wrench into the operation of all the other machines."[1] As a result, almost all economists need to account for the role of money and monetary policy at some stage when they address questions such as government spending and international trade.

The economist John Cochrane* highlights the importance of

> **❝[It was]** one of the decisive achievements of the post-war economics. **❞**
> Paul Krugman on Friedman's prediction of "stagflation"—the combination of rising unemployment* and rising inflation that affected the economies of the United States and Britain in the 1970s.

Friedman's ideas in contemporary debates in his essay "The Role of Monetary Policy Revisited." For example, he asks: "How many fallacies like the 1968 Phillips Curve* underlie our current policy experiments?"[2] More specifically, Cochrane notes that current monetary efforts to stimulate the economy such as "quantitative easing"*—the policy of a central bank buying financial assets from commercial banks—may be overly optimistic. In the case of the United States, recently, the US Federal Reserve's* policy of quantitative easing "exploded reserves from $50 billion to $3 trillion. Despite that, [gross domestic product*] has yet to really recover from the recession. You have to question, is this doing any good at all? It's time to think like Friedman and evaluate all these policies, while demanding a basis in clear and simple theories."[3]

Interaction

Many of Friedman's ideas have been fully merged into modern economics, and many of those that have not are currently out of favor. For example, there is little intellectual desire to revisit Friedman's constant money-supply* hypothesis.

With that in mind, much of the critical debate around Friedman's impact deals with his political positions and the use of his policies internationally. Many of Friedman's critics are on the left politically, and challenge his promotion of free markets, both in the United States and elsewhere. In part this is due to Friedman's complex identity. Paul Krugman* writes that Friedman took on three roles in his life: the role of "economist's economist," the role of a policy pioneer for monetarism, and the role of "Friedman the ideologue, the great popularizer of free-market doctrine."[4] While the last of these is responsible for most of the criticism he has received, Friedman has been certainly been criticized for his advocacy of monetarism too.

Krugman has also examined the uneven relationship between Friedman and the political right in America: "Friedman, it turns out, was too nuanced and realist a figure for the modern right, which doesn't do nuance and rejects reality."[5] While embracing Friedman in this limited way, Krugman maintains his distance: "I'd argue that the experience of the past 15 years, first in Japan and now across the Western world, shows that Keynes* was right and Friedman was wrong about the ability of unaided monetary policy to fight depressions.* The truth is that we need a more activist government than Friedman was willing to [accept]."[6]

This comment captures Friedman's current place in political and economic debate. To some he is seen as a right-wing villain; to others, a libertarian* hero. But the practical nature of a number of his ideas offers the opportunity for a more nuanced opinion.

The Continuing Debate

Some of Friedman's challengers have suggested that while he may have been well meaning, his proposals have been unsuccessful. In "Milton Friedman: a Study in Failure," an essay published just after Friedman's death, Richard Adams, the Education editor for the British newspaper the *Guardian*, argues that despite his reputation as a great economist, most of Friedman's ideas, including key parts of monetarism, have been political and economic failures.[7] Adams points out that Friedman's proposal that central banks should set fixed rules for growth of the money supply was tried in the 1970s and 1980s, but it was found to be unsuccessful and abandoned. "Today, no major central bank directly targets money supply data in setting monetary policy—instead they are far more pragmatic."[8]

Other critics, most notably the writer Naomi Klein,* have challenged Friedman on moral grounds. Referring to Friedman's advisory role in the overhaul of the Chilean economy in the mid-1970s after the right-wing military coup, which she calls "the most extreme capitalism makeover anywhere," Klein suggests that the "rapid-fire transformation of the economy" was an unneeded "shock." Moreover, she says, it was motivated by support for free enterprise rather than a desire to promote social good.[9] Klein's critique is typical of the view of Friedman as the public face of free-market ideology, and the mastermind behind the widespread privatization of public institutions in developing countries in the 1970s and 1980s. Klein describes him as the "grand guru of unfettered capitalism" and credits him with "writing the rulebook for the contemporary, hyper-mobile global economy."

NOTES

1   Milton Friedman, "The Role of Monetary Policy," *American Economic Review* 58, no. 1 (March 1, 1968): 12.

2   John Cochrane, "The Role of Monetary Policy Revisited," accessed February 18, 2015, http://bfi.uchicago.edu/feature-story/role-monetary-policy-revisited.

3   Cochrane, "The Role."

4   Paul Krugman, "Who Was Milton Friedman?" accessed February 18, 2015, http://www.nybooks.com/articles/archives/2007/feb/15/who-was-milton-friedman/.

5   Paul Krugman, "Milton Friedman, Unperson," accessed February 18, 2015, http://www.nytimes.com/2013/08/12/opinion/krugman-milton-friedman-unperson.html?smid=tw-share&_r=0.

6   Krugman, "Milton Friedman, Unperson."

7   Richard Adams, "Milton Friedman: A Study in Failure," *Guardian*, accessed February 18, 2015, http://www.theguardian.com/commentisfree/2006/nov/16/post650.

8   Adams, "Milton Friedman."

9   Klein, *The Shock Doctrine*, accessed February 18, 2015, http://www.naomiklein.org/shock-doctrine/excerpt.

WHERE NEXT?

KEY POINTS

- The text remains the starting point for discussions on the role of monetary policy* in broader macroeconomic* stability.

- The tools central banks have at their disposal have expanded, as have the temptations to become involved in broader economic fine-tuning. But there remains the central question of whether short-term gains are outweighed by potential long-term consequences.

- Friedman's text, laying bare the dangers of an overly activist monetary policy, was key to the twentieth century's push back against "excessive" government intervention in the economy.

Potential

The financial crisis of 2008–10* highlighted the continuing instability of the market economy. It also showed how monetary policymakers are constantly trying to adapt to new information and understandings of how the economy works. It is hard to say how exactly monetary policy will evolve over the coming century, but two points seem reasonably clear. First, Friedman forever changed how monetary authorities view their role in providing a stable foundation for the economy. Second, Friedman's proposal for a fixed rate of monetary growth is unlikely to be tried again, since there is a clear need to use monetary policy to smooth out economic fluctuations (by adjusting the money supply,* as needed).

As the economist John Cochrane* notes, Friedman's paper will likely remain important in the future as a reminder of the limitations

> **❝**Monetary policy cannot achieve by itself what a broader and more balanced set of economic policies might achieve; in particular, it cannot neutralize the fiscal and financial risks that the country faces. It certainly cannot fine-tune economic outcomes.**❞**
> Benjamin Bernanke, US Federal Reserve Chairman

of intervention. As management of the economy becomes ever more complex, these lessons will only become more relevant.

Consider, for example, the role of monetary policy in an age when national governments have enormous debt: "Every year [the US] takes in $2.5 trillion and spends $3.5 trillion. We bear an existing debt of $16 trillion, and owe a gazillion dollars in future promises," says Cochrane. "If the Fed decides to tighten monetary policy and set interest rates to 5 percent, on $16 trillion in debt that adds $800 billion a year to the deficit." As the conditions of the economy change and present new challenges for policymakers, "The Role" will serve as a reference point for the lesson that "monetary policy can harm the economy" and that policymakers must tread carefully.[1]

Future Directions
One of the economists whose approach to monetary policy somewhat mirrors Friedman's is Raghuram Rajan,* currently serving as the governor of the Reserve Bank of India, that country's central bank. Like Friedman, Rajan's views are motivated by a strong belief in free markets* and skepticism of fiscal policy* (that is, government spending to stimulate the economy). In response to the financial crisis of 2008–10, for example, Rajan argued for fundamental economic changes such as training more people for the jobs in the new global economy, making the tax structure more favorable to business start-ups, and so on, rather than governmental stimulus programs:

"Today's economic troubles are not simply the result of inadequate demand but the result, equally, of [an environment that is not favorable enough to business and economic growth]. For decades before the financial crisis in 2008, advanced economies were losing their ability to grow by making useful things."[2]

In this contemporary version of a debate between Keynesians[*] arguing for fiscal stimulus[*] and free-market supporters arguing for changes to economic fundamentals, Rajan plays the role of Friedman.

Another economist who has shown an approach similar to Friedman's is Naranya Kocherlakota,[*] currently president of the Minneapolis Federal Reserve—though Friedman and Kocherlakota may not have agreed on principles. In a move that might remind us of Friedman's support for a monetary policy in which gradual price changes are the goal, Kocherlakota has argued that the Federal Reserve[*] must be more clear about its expectations for meeting its inflation goals. In a recent address, for example, Kocherlakota argued that "price stability" requires a clear explanation of the Fed's timeline for achieving inflation targets.[3]

Summary

"The Role of Monetary Policy" remains a work of extraordinary originality and insight, offering the power to predict future developments. It successfully challenged—and overturned—the theoretical basis of the Keynesian approach that was widely accepted up to then. And it changed the course of monetary policy over the following decades, allowing policymakers to learn from previous mistakes and not worsen economic problems and crises. For these reasons it will continue to be important for both policymakers and students of economics.

It is the strength of Friedman's critical analysis of Keynesian economics that sets his paper apart from other academic work. In a short article of 17 pages, Friedman forcefully challenged the theoretical foundations of decades of policymaking and established the basis for the monetarist school of thought. He changed many widely held assumptions for good.

Readers of the paper will gain insight into the historical evolution of monetary policy in America, as well as an outstanding example of economic analysis. Whereas many economics papers are highly technical and somewhat abstract, "The Role" will prepare people to think about events in the financial press and to better understand the world around them. Further, as Friedman is one of the most important economists of the last century, reading the paper will expose students to some of the most basic questions in the public debate around economics: how important is the government to economic policy, and what kinds of policies can work?

NOTES

1   John Cochrane, "The Role of Monetary Policy Revisited," accessed February 18, 2015, http://bfi.uchicago.edu/feature-story/role-monetary-policy-revisited.

2   Raghuram Rajan, "The True Lessons of the Financial Crisis," *Foreign Affairs*, accessed February 18, 2015, http://www.foreignaffairs.com/articles/134863/raghuram-g-rajan/the-true-lessons-of-the-recession.

3   Naranya Kocherlakota, "Clarifying the Meaning of Price Stability," accessed February 18, 2015, https://www.minneapolisfed.org/publications/the-region/clarifying-the-meaning-of-price-stability.

GLOSSARIES

GLOSSARY OF TERMS

Aggregate demand: a term for the total demand for goods and services in the economy at a given time.

Business cycle: an economic notion describing ups and downs in the economy over a period of several years due to alternating phases of boom (growth) and bust (contraction). These expansions and contractions of the economy tend to seesaw around the economy's long-term growth trend.

Capitalism: an economic system in which industry and trade are controlled by private citizens with property rights over their goods and services. The forum in which trade takes place is the marketplace.

Chicago school: a cluster of economists based around the University of Chicago. It is generally characterized by a belief in neoclassical economics, specifically price theory, and a general belief in the power of markets.

Classical tradition in economics: the first modern school of economic thought, most often associated with Adam Smith, David Ricardo, Thomas Malthus, and John Stuart Mill. The tradition was active from the late eighteenth century to the mid- to late-nineteenth century. Classical economists generally believed markets to be self-regulating.

Consumer choice: the different products and services that are available to the general buying public.

Consumption: an economic concept that refers to the aggregate (overall) purchasing behavior in the economy.

Deflation: the phenomenon of too little money chasing too many goods, resulting in declining prices.

Depression: a sustained downturn in the economy, typically defined in the United States as a decline in gross domestic product exceeding 10 percent or a recession lasting at least two years.

Division of labor: the specialization of cooperating individuals who perform specific tasks as part of a production process.

Economic growth: the increase in output of goods and services that an economy produces over a certain period of time.

Economic indicators: measurable features of an economy such as inflation or unemployment, expressed as a statistics.

Exchange rate: the rate at which you can exchange one currency for another.

Federal Reserve: the central banking system of the United States, which regulates the US monetary and financial system.

Financial crisis of 2008–10: an economic crisis that originated in the United States and spread through much of Europe and beyond. It is considered to be the most significant financial crisis since the Great Depression of the 1930s.

Fiscal policy: the use of governmental spending to influence the economy. Examples include spending on social programs, taxation, and the financing of basic public works projects such as highways and bridges.

Fiscal stimulus: the policy of increasing governmental expenditure by increasing consumption or lowering taxes, usually with the goal of decreasing unemployment and stimulating economic growth.

Free market: a system in which goods and services are exchanged in a marketplace mediated by the price system. Free markets are most often distinguished from centrally planned economies.

Free trade: the policy of not restricting the exchange of goods and services between countries. The opposite of free trade is when tariffs restrict the import and export of goods and services.

Great Depression: the longest and most severe depression of the twentieth century. It originated in the United States, with the collapse in stock prices in late 1929. Unemployment in the USA reached 25 percent, while other countries saw it rise above 30 percent. In many countries, a prolonged recovery did not occur until the end of World War II.

Gross domestic product and **gross national product:** GDP, a leading economic indicator, is the market value of all goods and services within a country's borders at a given time. GNP is the market value of goods and services produced by citizens of a country in a given period, regardless of location. The output of an American-owned factory in Kenya, for example, would be included in the US GNP, but not the US GDP.

Growth rate: an increase that is usually measured in periods of time.

Ideologue: a person who adheres to a particular ideology or doctrine and is firmly entrenched in their position.

Inflation: the phenomenon of too much money chasing too few goods, resulting in rising prices.

Interest rate: the cost of borrowing money. The Federal Reserve controls interest rates through the "federal funds rate," or the interest rate for federal funds.

Jewish: describing a follower of Judaism, a monotheistic religion founded over 3,500 years ago in the Middle East. Today Jews are largely concentrated in Israel and the United States, with smaller populations in dozens of other countries around the world.

Keynesianism: a school of economic thought that argues that economic markets are not self-correcting. It suggests that activist government policies can help to stabilize the economy through government spending (fiscal policy) and control of the supply of money (monetary policy).

Laissez-faire: a concept in economics describing the situation in which governments do not intervene in the economy and let markets take their own course.

Left wing: the part of a political system or party that is traditionally socialist or reforming.

Libertarianism: a school of political thought that calls for near absolute freedom of individual action with a minimal role for government interference.

Macroeconomics: the branch of economics that deals with the performance of the economy as a whole.

Mercantilism: an economic regime practiced in Europe from the sixteenth to the eighteenth century that forbid free trade between countries and encouraged governments to accumulate resources at the expense of their rivals. Adam Smith's *Wealth of Nations*, which argues the benefits of free trade, was a rebuttal of this position.

Microeconomics: the branch of economics that deals with decision-making processes at the level of individuals and firms.

Monetarism: an economic viewpoint that argues that in the short run adjusting the money supply can have a significant impact on economic outcomes such as unemployment, while in the long run it cannot. The monetarism position emphasizes the differences between real and nominal prices, and argues that monetary policy should follow a rulebook to create stable expectations about the economy.

Monetary economics: the branch of economics that studies the function of money in the economy. A key question of monetary economics is the relationship between various monetary aggregates, such as the money supply, and economic variables, such as employment.

Monetary policy: the mechanism used to control the supply of money within an economic zone. A policy that increases the money supply is "expansionary," while a policy that decreases it is "contractionary." Monetary authorities pursue policies that maintain stable prices and keep unemployment low. It differs from fiscal policy, which is linked to taxation, government spending, and borrowing.

Money supply: an economic concept generally defined as the total monetary assets in the economy at a given time.

New Keynesianism: a school in economics that combines aspects of rational expectations, classical economics, and Keynesian theory.

Nobel Prize in Economics: also known as the Sveriges Riksbank Prize in Economic Sciences, this is a highly prestigious award given annually to an economist who has made a significant contribution to the subject.

Nominal values: in economics, nominal values are expressed in historical terms, while real values are adjusted to reflect price and other changes over time. For example, the nominal price of a car in 1930 was much less than the nominal price today, but the real price, in terms of purchasing power, was likely higher.

Permanent income hypothesis: the idea that consumption (that is, spending on goods and services) in any period is related both to a person's *present* income and their expected *future* income.

Phillips curve: a measure of the relationship between the rate of inflation and the rate of unemployment. It observed that lower unemployment correlates with a higher rate of inflation, suggesting that there is a trade-off between the two.

Price level: an index or measure of overall prices in the economy. Changes in the price level are determined by the rate of inflation.

Price theory: a theory in economics based on the idea that the value of a good or service can be determined by the relationship between its supply and demand.

Purchasing power: the number of goods and services that can be bought with a given unit of currency.

Quantitative easing: a monetary policy in which the central bank purchases financial assets from commercial banks, raising the price of those assets and stimulating the monetary base.

Rational expectations: an economic theory based on the assumption that economic agents make accurate, rational predictions about the future.

Real values: in economics, nominal values are expressed in historical terms, while real values are adjusted to reflect price and other changes over time. For example, the nominal price of a car in 1930 was much less than the nominal price today, but the real price, in terms of purchasing power, was likely higher.

Scarcity: the economic problem posed by limited resources and unlimited wants. Economists only study scarce resources, as unlimited resources have no inherent economic value.

Stagflation: an economic term that refers to the situation when high inflation and high unemployment occur simultaneously.

Stock market: an exchange where financial stocks, shares, and bonds are traded.

Unemployment: the state that occurs when people who are seeking work cannot find it.

World War II: a global war from 1939 to 1945 centered in Europe and the Pacific. It was fought between the Allies (United States, Britain, Soviet Union, and others) and the Axis (Germany, Italy, Japan, and others).

PEOPLE MENTIONED IN THE TEXT

Ben Bernanke (b. 1953) is an American economist and chairman of the US Federal Reserve—the most powerful monetary policy-making role in the world.

Karl Brunner (1916–89) was a Swiss economist who was a key member of the monetarist school of economics and a frequent critic of the Federal Reserve System.

Willem Buiter (b. 1949) is an American-British economist known for his work on monetary economics.

John Cochrane (b. 1957) is an American economist who is best known for his work linking finance and macroeconomics.*

Bradford Delong (b. 1960) is an American economist who has made contributions to monetary economics and economic history and is perhaps best known as a prominent blogger.

Irving Fisher (1867–1947) was an American economist. He has been described as a neoclassical economist—a school of economics based on three core assumptions: People are rational and have discernible preferences based on value; people maximize utility, while firms maximize profits; people act with full and relevant information. He is credited with beginning the school of macroeconomics known as "monetarism."

Gottfried Haberler (1900–95) was an Austrian-American economist associated with the Austrian School of Economics, who is perhaps best known for his ideas related to comparative advantage and trade.

Kevin Hoover (b. 1955) is an American economist who has studied the philosophy and methodology of economics with a particular emphasis on causation.

Harry Johnson (1923–77) was a Canadian economist whose work focused on international trade and international finance. He is associated with the monetarist school of economics.

John Maynard Keynes (1883–1946) was a British economist whose contributions to the theory of macroeconomics were greatly influential to economic policy. He argued against the leading ideas of his day, that economic slowdowns are caused by a lack of aggregate (total) demand, and that at such times, governments should step in to promote demand by increasing their spending in the economy.

Naomi Klein (b. 1970) is a Canadian author best known for her books such as *The Shock Doctrine* and *No Logo*, challenging the foundations of global capitalism.

Naranya Kocherlakota (b. 1963) is an American economist who is currently President of the Federal Reserve Bank of Minneapolis. He is notable for changing his views on monetary policy during the financial crisis of 2008–2010.

Paul Krugman (b. 1953) is an American economist whose work on international trade earned him a Nobel Prize in 2008. He is also widely known as a commentator on politics and economics for the *New York Times*.

Robert Lucas (b. 1937) is an American economist known for developing the rational expectations approach to economics and for his association with the Chicago School of Economics.

Erik Lundberg (1907–87) was a Swedish economist who served as chairman of the Economics Prize Committee that selects the winner of the Nobel Prize in Economics from 1975 to 1979.

Gregory Mankiw (b. 1958) is an American macroeconomist known as the author of a popular undergraduate economics textbook, *Principles of Economics*. As a public servant in the United States, Mankiw was the chairman of the Council of Economic Advisors from 2003 to 2005 under President George W. Bush.

Karl Marx (1818–83) was a German philosopher whose works *Capital* and *The Communist Manifesto* form the intellectual basis for communism.

Bennett McCallum (b. 1935) is an American economist whose work applies statistical methods to monetary economics.

William McChesney Martin Jr. (1951–98) was an American politician who served as chairman of the Federal Reserve Bank from 1951 to 1970. He served under five different American presidents.

Allan Meltzer (b. 1928) is an American economist in the monetarist tradition, who from 2012 to 2014 served as president of the Mount Pelerin Society, an organization dedicated to political and economic freedom.

Edmund Phelps (b. 1933) is an American economist renowned for his work on the sources of economic growth, the savings rate, and price–wage dynamics, leading to his development of the natural rate of unemployment. He was awarded the 2006 Nobel Prize in Economics.

William Phillips (1914–75) was an economist from New Zealand whose best-known contribution to economics is the discovery of a negative relationship between inflation and unemployment, known as the Phillips Curve.

Augusto Pinochet (1915–2006) was the 30th President of Chile who held office from 1974–1990 after overthrowing the elected president in a military coup. He is known for the privatization of the economy during his rule.

Raghuram Rajan (b. 1963) is an Indian economist and Governor of the Reserve Bank of India. His research areas include banking, corporate finance, and economic development.

Ronald Reagan (1911–2004) was the 40th President of the United States. As President, Reagan was known for "Reaganomics," a policy of cutting taxes, controlling the money supply, and deregulating the economy in order to increase growth.

Lionel Robbins (1898–1984) was a British economist who was known for his ongoing debate with John Maynard Keynes and for providing a popular definition of "economics."

Adolph Sabath (1866–1952) was an American politician who served in the House of Representatives, representing Illinois, from 1907 to his death.

Paul Samuelson (1915–2009) was an American economist who made significant contributions to macroeconomics and is considered by some the "father of modern economics."

Thomas Sargent (b. 1943) is an American economist who developed statistical techniques to study the rational expectations hypothesis.

Anna J. Schwartz (1915–2012) was an American economist. Her most famous work was her collaboration with Milton Friedman on *A Monetary History of the United States, 1867–1960*, which fundamentally changed the understanding of the causes of the Great Depression and monetary economics.

Robert Skidelsky (b 1939) is a British economic historian perhaps best known for his three-volume biography of John Maynard Keynes.

Adam Smith (1723–90) was a Scottish philosopher and political economist best known for his works *The Theory of Moral Sentiments* (1759) and *An Inquiry into the Nature and Causes of the Wealth of Nations* (1776); the latter is widely considered the first modern work of economics.

Robert Solow (b. 1924) is an American economist who helped develop the theory of economic growth, specifically the Solow growth model.

George Stigler (1911–91) was an economist at the University of Chicago. He is best known for his work on "regulatory capture"—the idea that interest groups use the regulatory powers of government to their advantage.

Margaret Thatcher (1925–2013) was a British politician and the only woman to have held the office of Prime Minister, a position she occupied from 1979 to 1990. She is associated with policies designed to limit state involvement in the economy and stimulate free enterprise.

James Tobin (1918–2002) was an American economist who made pioneering studies in finance and the uses of monetary and fiscal policy. He is most associated with the Keynesian school.

Knut Wicksell (1851–1926) was a Swedish economist. His most influential contribution was his theory of interest, and his work is considered fundamental to macroeconomics.

WORKS CITED

WORKS CITED

Adams, Richard. "Milton Friedman: A Study in Failure." *Guardian*. Accessed February 18, 2015. http://www.theguardian.com/commentisfree/2006/nov/16/post650.

Bernanke, Ben. "The Great Moderation." Presented at the Eastern Economic Association, Washington, DC, February 20, 2004. Accessed February 18, 2015. http://www.federalreserve.gov/BOARDDOCS/SPEECHES/2004/20040220/default.htm.

_____. "The Macroeconomics of the Great Depression: A Comparative Approach." *Journal of Money, Credit, and Banking* 27, no. 1 (1995): 1–28.

_____. "On Milton Friedman's Ninetieth Birthday." Accessed February 18, 2015. http://www.federalreserve.gov/boarddocs/Speeches/2002/20021108/default.htm.

_____. "Remarks." Accessed February 18, 2015. http://www.federalreserve.gov/boarddocs/Speeches/2002/20021108/default.htm.

Blinder, Alan. "Keynesian Economics." Library of Economics and Liberty. Accessed February 18, 2015. http://www.econlib.org/library/Enc/KeynesianEconomics.html.

Brunner, Karl and Allan Meltzer. "Friedman's Monetary Theory." *Journal of Political Economy* 80, no. 5 (1972): 837–51.

Cochrane, John. "The Role of Monetary Policy Revisited." Accessed February 18, 2015. http://bfi.uchicago.edu/feature-story/role-monetary-policy-revisited.

Delong, Bradford. "The Triumph of Monetarism?" *Journal of Economic Perspectives* 14, no. 1 (2000): 83–94.

Ebenstein, Lanny. *Milton Friedman: A Biography*. Basingstoke: Palgrave Macmillan, 2007.

"Federal Reserve Act of 1913." Accessed February 18, 2015. http://legisworks.org/sal/38/stats/STATUTE-38-Pg251a.pdf.

Fisher, Irving. *The Purchasing Power of Money*. New York: Cosimo Publishing, 2006.

Forder, James. "The Historical Place of the 'Friedman–Phelps' expectations critique." *The European Journal of the History of Economic Thought* 17, no. 3 (2010): 493–511.

Friedman, Milton, and Anna J. Schwartz. *A Monetary History of the United States, 1867–1960*. Princeton, NJ: Princeton University Press, 1963.

____. *A Theory of the Consumption Function*. Princeton, NJ: Princeton University Press: 1957.

Friedman, Milton. "Comments on the Critics." *Journal of Political Economy* 80 (1972): 906–50.

____."The Economy: We Are All Keynesians Now." *Time*, December 31, 1965.

____. "Inflation and Unemployment." Nobel Memorial Lecture, December 13, 1976. Accessed February 18, 2015. http://www.nobelprize.org/nobel_ prizes/economic-sciences/laureates/1976/friedman-lecture.pdf.

____. "Letter to General Pinochet on Our Return from Chile and His Reply." Accessed February 18, 2015. http://wwww.naomiklein.org/files/resources/ pdfs/friedman-pinochet-letters.pdf.

____. "The Role of Monetary Policy." *American Economic Review* 58, no. 1 (March 1968): 1–17.

Garrison, Roger. "Hayek and Friedman: Head to Head." Accessed February 18, 2015. http://www.auburn.edu/~garriro/hayek%20and%20friedman.pdf.

Hoover, Kevin. "Phillips Curve." Library of Economics and Liberty. Accessed February 18, 2015. http://www.econlib.org/library/Enc/PhillipsCurve.html.

"Interview with Milton Friedman." Public Broadcasting Service. Accessed February 18, 2015. http://www.pbs.org/wgbh/commandingheights/shared/ minitext/int_miltonfriedman.html#7.

Johnson, Harry. "The Keynesian Revolution and the Monetarist Counter-Revolution." *American Economic Review* 61, no. 2 (1971): 1–14.

Keynes, John Maynard. *General Theory of Employment, Interest, and Money.* Accessed February 18, 2015. http://cas.umkc.edu/economics/people/ facultypages/kregel/courses/econ645/winter2011/generaltheory.pdf.

Klein, Naomi. *The Shock Doctrine: The Rise of Disaster Capitalism*. Toronto: Knopf Canada, 2009.

Kocherlakota, Naranya. "Clarifying the Meaning of Price Stability." Accessed February 18, 2015. https://www.minneapolisfed.org/publications/the-region/ clarifying-the-meaning-of-price-stability.

Krugman, Paul. "Milton Friedman, Unperson." *New York Times.* Accessed February 18, 2015. http://www.nytimes.com/2013/08/12/opinion/krugman-milton-friedman-unperson.html?smid=tw-share&_r=0.

_____. "The Pigou Effect." Accessed February 18, 2015. http://krugman. blogs.nytimes.com/2013/08/10/the-pigou-effect-double-super-special-wonkish/.

_____. "Who Was Milton Friedman?" Accessed February 18, 2015. http:// www.nybooks.com/articles/archives/2007/feb/15/who-was-milton-friedman/.

Lucas, Robert. "Expectations and the Neutrality of Money." _Journal of Economic Theory_ 4 (1972): 103–24.

Mankiw, Gregory. "New Keynesian Economics." Library of Economics and Liberty. Accessed February 18, 2015. http://www.econlib.org/library/Enc/ NewKeynesianEconomics.html.

Marx, Karl. _Capital: A Critique of Political Economy._ Edited by Friedrich Engels. New York: Cosimo, 2007.

McCallum, Bennett. "Monetarism." Library of Economics and Liberty. Accessed February 18, 2015. http://www.econlib.org/library/Enc/ Monetarism.html.

"Milton Friedman." Library of Economics and Liberty. Accessed February 18, 2015. http://www.econlib.org/library/Enc/bios/Friedman.html.

"Milton Friedman—Biographical." Nobelprize.org. Accessed February 18, 2015. http://www.nobelprize.org-/nobel_prizes/economics/laureates/1976/ friedman-autobio.html.

"Milton Friedman—Facts." Nobelprize.org. Accessed February 18, 2015. http://www.nobelprize.org/nobel_prizes/economic-sciences/laureates/1976/ friedman-facts.html.

"Milton Friedman, a Giant among Economists." _The Economist_, November 23, 2006.

Nelson, Edward. "Milton Friedman and US Monetary History: 1961–2006." Federal Reserve Bank of St. Louis, Working Paper Series (2007). Accessed February 18, 2015. http://research.stlouisfed.org/wp/2007/2007-002.pdf.

Phelps, Edmund. "Phillips Curves, Expectations of Inflation and Optimal Employment over Time." _Economica_ 34, no. 135 (1967): 254–81.

Phillips, Alban. "The Relation between Unemployment and the Rate of Change of Money Wage Rates in the United Kingdom, 1861–1957." _Economica_ 25, no. 100 (1958): 283–99.

Rajan, Raghuram. "The True Lessons of the Financial Crisis." _Foreign Affairs_. Accessed February 18, 2015. http://www.foreignaffairs.com/ articles/134863/raghuram-g-rajan/the-true-lessons-of-the-recession.

Robbins, Lionel. *An Essay on the Nature and Significance of Economic Science*. London: Macmillan, 1932.

Samuelson, Paul and Robert Solow. "Analytical Aspects of Anti-Inflation Policy." *American Economic Review* 50, no. 2 (1960): 177–94.

Sargent, Thomas. "Rational Expectations." Library of Economics and Liberty. Accessed February 18, 2015. http://www.econlib.org/library/Enc/RationalExpectations.html.

Smith, Adam. *An Inquiry into the Nature and Causes of the Wealth of Nations: A Selected Edition*. Oxford: Oxford University Press, 1998.

Snowdon, Brian, and Howard R. Vane. *Modern Macroeconomics: Its Origins, Development and Current State*. Cheltenham: Edward Elgar, 2005.

Tobin, James. "Inflation and Unemployment." *American Economic Review* 62, no. 1 (1972): 1–18.

Williamson, Stephen. "Kocherlakota: A Puzzle." *New Monetarism*. Accessed February 18, 2015. http://newmonetarism.blogspot.com/2013/09/kocherlakota-puzzle.html.

THE MACAT LIBRARY
BY DISCIPLINE

AFRICANA STUDIES

Chinua Achebe's *An Image of Africa: Racism in Conrad's Heart of Darkness*
W. E. B. Du Bois's *The Souls of Black Folk*
Zora Neale Huston's *Characteristics of Negro Expression*
Martin Luther King Jr's *Why We Can't Wait*
Toni Morrison's *Playing in the Dark: Whiteness in the American Literary Imagination*

ANTHROPOLOGY

Arjun Appadurai's *Modernity at Large: Cultural Dimensions of Globalisation*
Philippe Ariès's *Centuries of Childhood*
Franz Boas's *Race, Language and Culture*
Kim Chan & Renée Mauborgne's *Blue Ocean Strategy*
Jared Diamond's *Guns, Germs & Steel: the Fate of Human Societies*
Jared Diamond's *Collapse: How Societies Choose to Fail or Survive*
E. E. Evans-Pritchard's *Witchcraft, Oracles and Magic Among the Azande*
James Ferguson's *The Anti-Politics Machine*
Clifford Geertz's *The Interpretation of Cultures*
David Graeber's *Debt: the First 5000 Years*
Karen Ho's *Liquidated: An Ethnography of Wall Street*
Geert Hofstede's *Culture's Consequences: Comparing Values, Behaviors, Institutes and Organizations across Nations*
Claude Lévi-Strauss's *Structural Anthropology*
Jay Macleod's *Ain't No Makin' It: Aspirations and Attainment in a Low-Income Neighborhood*
Saba Mahmood's *The Politics of Piety: The Islamic Revival and the Feminist Subject*
Marcel Mauss's *The Gift*

BUSINESS

Jean Lave & Etienne Wenger's *Situated Learning*
Theodore Levitt's *Marketing Myopia*
Burton G. Malkiel's *A Random Walk Down Wall Street*
Douglas McGregor's *The Human Side of Enterprise*
Michael Porter's *Competitive Strategy: Creating and Sustaining Superior Performance*
John Kotter's *Leading Change*
C. K. Prahalad & Gary Hamel's *The Core Competence of the Corporation*

CRIMINOLOGY

Michelle Alexander's *The New Jim Crow: Mass Incarceration in the Age of Colorblindness*
Michael R. Gottfredson & Travis Hirschi's *A General Theory of Crime*
Richard Herrnstein & Charles A. Murray's *The Bell Curve: Intelligence and Class Structure in American Life*
Elizabeth Loftus's *Eyewitness Testimony*
Jay Macleod's *Ain't No Makin' It: Aspirations and Attainment in a Low-Income Neighborhood*
Philip Zimbardo's *The Lucifer Effect*

ECONOMICS

Janet Abu-Lughod's *Before European Hegemony*
Ha-Joon Chang's *Kicking Away the Ladder*
David Brion Davis's *The Problem of Slavery in the Age of Revolution*
Milton Friedman's *The Role of Monetary Policy*
Milton Friedman's *Capitalism and Freedom*
David Graeber's *Debt: the First 5000 Years*
Friedrich Hayek's *The Road to Serfdom*
Karen Ho's *Liquidated: An Ethnography of Wall Street*

John Maynard Keynes's *The General Theory of Employment, Interest and Money*
Charles P. Kindleberger's *Manias, Panics and Crashes*
Robert Lucas's *Why Doesn't Capital Flow from Rich to Poor Countries?*
Burton G. Malkiel's *A Random Walk Down Wall Street*
Thomas Robert Malthus's *An Essay on the Principle of Population*
Karl Marx's *Capital*
Thomas Piketty's *Capital in the Twenty-First Century*
Amartya Sen's *Development as Freedom*
Adam Smith's *The Wealth of Nations*
Nassim Nicholas Taleb's *The Black Swan: The Impact of the Highly Improbable*
Amos Tversky's & Daniel Kahneman's *Judgment under Uncertainty: Heuristics and Biases*
Mahbub Ul Haq's *Reflections on Human Development*
Max Weber's *The Protestant Ethic and the Spirit of Capitalism*

FEMINISM AND GENDER STUDIES

Judith Butler's *Gender Trouble*
Simone De Beauvoir's *The Second Sex*
Michel Foucault's *History of Sexuality*
Betty Friedan's *The Feminine Mystique*
Saba Mahmood's *The Politics of Piety: The Islamic Revival and the Feminist Subject*
Joan Wallach Scott's *Gender and the Politics of History*
Mary Wollstonecraft's *A Vindication of the Rights of Woman*
Virginia Woolf's *A Room of One's Own*

GEOGRAPHY

The Brundtland Report's *Our Common Future*
Rachel Carson's *Silent Spring*
Charles Darwin's *On the Origin of Species*
James Ferguson's *The Anti-Politics Machine*
Jane Jacobs's *The Death and Life of Great American Cities*
James Lovelock's *Gaia: A New Look at Life on Earth*
Amartya Sen's *Development as Freedom*
Mathis Wackernagel & William Rees's *Our Ecological Footprint*

HISTORY

Janet Abu-Lughod's *Before European Hegemony*
Benedict Anderson's *Imagined Communities*
Bernard Bailyn's *The Ideological Origins of the American Revolution*
Hanna Batatu's *The Old Social Classes And The Revolutionary Movements Of Iraq*
Christopher Browning's *Ordinary Men: Reserve Police Batallion 101 and the Final Solution in Poland*
Edmund Burke's *Reflections on the Revolution in France*
William Cronon's *Nature's Metropolis: Chicago And The Great West*
Alfred W. Crosby's *The Columbian Exchange*
Hamid Dabashi's *Iran: A People Interrupted*
David Brion Davis's *The Problem of Slavery in the Age of Revolution*
Nathalie Zemon Davis's *The Return of Martin Guerre*
Jared Diamond's *Guns, Germs & Steel: the Fate of Human Societies*
Frank Dikotter's *Mao's Great Famine*
John W Dower's *War Without Mercy: Race And Power In The Pacific War*
W. E. B. Du Bois's *The Souls of Black Folk*
Richard J. Evans's *In Defence of History*
Lucien Febvre's *The Problem of Unbelief in the 16th Century*
Sheila Fitzpatrick's *Everyday Stalinism*

Eric Foner's *Reconstruction: America's Unfinished Revolution, 1863-1877*
Michel Foucault's *Discipline and Punish*
Michel Foucault's *History of Sexuality*
Francis Fukuyama's *The End of History and the Last Man*
John Lewis Gaddis's *We Now Know: Rethinking Cold War History*
Ernest Gellner's *Nations and Nationalism*
Eugene Genovese's *Roll, Jordan, Roll: The World the Slaves Made*
Carlo Ginzburg's *The Night Battles*
Daniel Goldhagen's *Hitler's Willing Executioners*
Jack Goldstone's *Revolution and Rebellion in the Early Modern World*
Antonio Gramsci's *The Prison Notebooks*
Alexander Hamilton, John Jay & James Madison's *The Federalist Papers*
Christopher Hill's *The World Turned Upside Down*
Carole Hillenbrand's *The Crusades: Islamic Perspectives*
Thomas Hobbes's *Leviathan*
Eric Hobsbawm's *The Age Of Revolution*
John A. Hobson's *Imperialism: A Study*
Albert Hourani's *History of the Arab Peoples*
Samuel P. Huntington's *The Clash of Civilizations and the Remaking of World Order*
C. L. R. James's *The Black Jacobins*
Tony Judt's *Postwar: A History of Europe Since 1945*
Ernst Kantorowicz's *The King's Two Bodies: A Study in Medieval Political Theology*
Paul Kennedy's *The Rise and Fall of the Great Powers*
Ian Kershaw's *The "Hitler Myth": Image and Reality in the Third Reich*
John Maynard Keynes's *The General Theory of Employment, Interest and Money*
Charles P. Kindleberger's *Manias, Panics and Crashes*
Martin Luther King Jr's *Why We Can't Wait*
Henry Kissinger's *World Order: Reflections on the Character of Nations and the Course of History*
Thomas Kuhn's *The Structure of Scientific Revolutions*
Georges Lefebvre's *The Coming of the French Revolution*
John Locke's *Two Treatises of Government*
Niccolò Machiavelli's *The Prince*
Thomas Robert Malthus's *An Essay on the Principle of Population*
Mahmood Mamdani's *Citizen and Subject: Contemporary Africa And The Legacy Of Late Colonialism*
Karl Marx's *Capital*
Stanley Milgram's *Obedience to Authority*
John Stuart Mill's *On Liberty*
Thomas Paine's *Common Sense*
Thomas Paine's *Rights of Man*
Geoffrey Parker's *Global Crisis: War, Climate Change and Catastrophe in the Seventeenth Century*
Jonathan Riley-Smith's *The First Crusade and the Idea of Crusading*
Jean-Jacques Rousseau's *The Social Contract*
Joan Wallach Scott's *Gender and the Politics of History*
Theda Skocpol's *States and Social Revolutions*
Adam Smith's *The Wealth of Nations*
Timothy Snyder's *Bloodlands: Europe Between Hitler and Stalin*
Sun Tzu's *The Art of War*
Keith Thomas's *Religion and the Decline of Magic*
Thucydides's *The History of the Peloponnesian War*
Frederick Jackson Turner's *The Significance of the Frontier in American History*
Odd Arne Westad's *The Global Cold War: Third World Interventions And The Making Of Our Times*

The Macat Library By Discipline

LITERATURE

Chinua Achebe's *An Image of Africa: Racism in Conrad's Heart of Darkness*
Roland Barthes's *Mythologies*
Homi K. Bhabha's *The Location of Culture*
Judith Butler's *Gender Trouble*
Simone De Beauvoir's *The Second Sex*
Ferdinand De Saussure's *Course in General Linguistics*
T. S. Eliot's *The Sacred Wood: Essays on Poetry and Criticism*
Zora Neale Huston's *Characteristics of Negro Expression*
Toni Morrison's *Playing in the Dark: Whiteness in the American Literary Imagination*
Edward Said's *Orientalism*
Gayatri Chakravorty Spivak's *Can the Subaltern Speak?*
Mary Wollstonecraft's *A Vindication of the Rights of Women*
Virginia Woolf's *A Room of One's Own*

PHILOSOPHY

Elizabeth Anscombe's *Modern Moral Philosophy*
Hannah Arendt's *The Human Condition*
Aristotle's *Metaphysics*
Aristotle's *Nicomachean Ethics*
Edmund Gettier's *Is Justified True Belief Knowledge?*
Georg Wilhelm Friedrich Hegel's *Phenomenology of Spirit*
David Hume's *Dialogues Concerning Natural Religion*
David Hume's *The Enquiry for Human Understanding*
Immanuel Kant's *Religion within the Boundaries of Mere Reason*
Immanuel Kant's *Critique of Pure Reason*
Søren Kierkegaard's *The Sickness Unto Death*
Søren Kierkegaard's *Fear and Trembling*
C. S. Lewis's *The Abolition of Man*
Alasdair MacIntyre's *After Virtue*
Marcus Aurelius's *Meditations*
Friedrich Nietzsche's *On the Genealogy of Morality*
Friedrich Nietzsche's *Beyond Good and Evil*
Plato's *Republic*
Plato's *Symposium*
Jean-Jacques Rousseau's *The Social Contract*
Gilbert Ryle's *The Concept of Mind*
Baruch Spinoza's *Ethics*
Sun Tzu's *The Art of War*
Ludwig Wittgenstein's *Philosophical Investigations*

POLITICS

Benedict Anderson's *Imagined Communities*
Aristotle's *Politics*
Bernard Bailyn's *The Ideological Origins of the American Revolution*
Edmund Burke's *Reflections on the Revolution in France*
John C. Calhoun's *A Disquisition on Government*
Ha-Joon Chang's *Kicking Away the Ladder*
Hamid Dabashi's *Iran: A People Interrupted*
Hamid Dabashi's *Theology of Discontent: The Ideological Foundation of the Islamic Revolution in Iran*
Robert Dahl's *Democracy and its Critics*
Robert Dahl's *Who Governs?*
David Brion Davis's *The Problem of Slavery in the Age of Revolution*

Alexis De Tocqueville's *Democracy in America*
James Ferguson's *The Anti-Politics Machine*
Frank Dikotter's *Mao's Great Famine*
Sheila Fitzpatrick's *Everyday Stalinism*
Eric Foner's *Reconstruction: America's Unfinished Revolution, 1863-1877*
Milton Friedman's *Capitalism and Freedom*
Francis Fukuyama's *The End of History and the Last Man*
John Lewis Gaddis's *We Now Know: Rethinking Cold War History*
Ernest Gellner's *Nations and Nationalism*
David Graeber's *Debt: the First 5000 Years*
Antonio Gramsci's *The Prison Notebooks*
Alexander Hamilton, John Jay & James Madison's *The Federalist Papers*
Friedrich Hayek's *The Road to Serfdom*
Christopher Hill's *The World Turned Upside Down*
Thomas Hobbes's *Leviathan*
John A. Hobson's *Imperialism: A Study*
Samuel P. Huntington's *The Clash of Civilizations and the Remaking of World Order*
Tony Judt's *Postwar: A History of Europe Since 1945*
David C. Kang's *China Rising: Peace, Power and Order in East Asia*
Paul Kennedy's *The Rise and Fall of Great Powers*
Robert Keohane's *After Hegemony*
Martin Luther King Jr.'s *Why We Can't Wait*
Henry Kissinger's *World Order: Reflections on the Character of Nations and the Course of History*
John Locke's *Two Treatises of Government*
Niccolò Machiavelli's *The Prince*
Thomas Robert Malthus's *An Essay on the Principle of Population*
Mahmood Mamdani's *Citizen and Subject: Contemporary Africa And The Legacy Of Late Colonialism*
Karl Marx's *Capital*
John Stuart Mill's *On Liberty*
John Stuart Mill's *Utilitarianism*
Hans Morgenthau's *Politics Among Nations*
Thomas Paine's *Common Sense*
Thomas Paine's *Rights of Man*
Thomas Piketty's *Capital in the Twenty-First Century*
Robert D. Putman's *Bowling Alone*
John Rawls's *Theory of Justice*
Jean-Jacques Rousseau's *The Social Contract*
Theda Skocpol's *States and Social Revolutions*
Adam Smith's *The Wealth of Nations*
Sun Tzu's *The Art of War*
Henry David Thoreau's *Civil Disobedience*
Thucydides's *The History of the Peloponnesian War*
Kenneth Waltz's *Theory of International Politics*
Max Weber's *Politics as a Vocation*
Odd Arne Westad's *The Global Cold War: Third World Interventions And The Making Of Our Times*

POSTCOLONIAL STUDIES

Roland Barthes's *Mythologies*
Frantz Fanon's *Black Skin, White Masks*
Homi K. Bhabha's *The Location of Culture*
Gustavo Gutiérrez's *A Theology of Liberation*
Edward Said's *Orientalism*
Gayatri Chakravorty Spivak's *Can the Subaltern Speak?*

The Macat Library By Discipline

PSYCHOLOGY

Gordon Allport's *The Nature of Prejudice*
Alan Baddeley & Graham Hitch's *Aggression: A Social Learning Analysis*
Albert Bandura's *Aggression: A Social Learning Analysis*
Leon Festinger's *A Theory of Cognitive Dissonance*
Sigmund Freud's *The Interpretation of Dreams*
Betty Friedan's *The Feminine Mystique*
Michael R. Gottfredson & Travis Hirschi's *A General Theory of Crime*
Eric Hoffer's *The True Believer: Thoughts on the Nature of Mass Movements*
William James's *Principles of Psychology*
Elizabeth Loftus's *Eyewitness Testimony*
A. H. Maslow's *A Theory of Human Motivation*
Stanley Milgram's *Obedience to Authority*
Steven Pinker's *The Better Angels of Our Nature*
Oliver Sacks's *The Man Who Mistook His Wife For a Hat*
Richard Thaler & Cass Sunstein's *Nudge: Improving Decisions About Health, Wealth and Happiness*
Amos Tversky's *Judgment under Uncertainty: Heuristics and Biases*
Philip Zimbardo's *The Lucifer Effect*

SCIENCE

Rachel Carson's *Silent Spring*
William Cronon's *Nature's Metropolis: Chicago And The Great West*
Alfred W. Crosby's *The Columbian Exchange*
Charles Darwin's *On the Origin of Species*
Richard Dawkin's *The Selfish Gene*
Thomas Kuhn's *The Structure of Scientific Revolutions*
Geoffrey Parker's *Global Crisis: War, Climate Change and Catastrophe in the Seventeenth Century*
Mathis Wackernagel & William Rees's *Our Ecological Footprint*

SOCIOLOGY

Michelle Alexander's *The New Jim Crow: Mass Incarceration in the Age of Colorblindness*
Gordon Allport's *The Nature of Prejudice*
Albert Bandura's *Aggression: A Social Learning Analysis*
Hanna Batatu's *The Old Social Classes And The Revolutionary Movements Of Iraq*
Ha-Joon Chang's *Kicking Away the Ladder*
W. E. B. Du Bois's *The Souls of Black Folk*
Émile Durkheim's *On Suicide*
Frantz Fanon's *Black Skin, White Masks*
Frantz Fanon's *The Wretched of the Earth*
Eric Foner's *Reconstruction: America's Unfinished Revolution, 1863-1877*
Eugene Genovese's *Roll, Jordan, Roll: The World the Slaves Made*
Jack Goldstone's *Revolution and Rebellion in the Early Modern World*
Antonio Gramsci's *The Prison Notebooks*
Richard Herrnstein & Charles A Murray's *The Bell Curve: Intelligence and Class Structure in American Life*
Eric Hoffer's *The True Believer: Thoughts on the Nature of Mass Movements*
Jane Jacobs's *The Death and Life of Great American Cities*
Robert Lucas's *Why Doesn't Capital Flow from Rich to Poor Countries?*
Jay Macleod's *Ain't No Makin' It: Aspirations and Attainment in a Low Income Neighborhood*
Elaine May's *Homeward Bound: American Families in the Cold War Era*
Douglas McGregor's *The Human Side of Enterprise*
C. Wright Mills's *The Sociological Imagination*

Thomas Piketty's *Capital in the Twenty-First Century*
Robert D. Putman's *Bowling Alone*
David Riesman's *The Lonely Crowd: A Study of the Changing American Character*
Edward Said's *Orientalism*
Joan Wallach Scott's *Gender and the Politics of History*
Theda Skocpol's *States and Social Revolutions*
Max Weber's *The Protestant Ethic and the Spirit of Capitalism*

THEOLOGY

Augustine's *Confessions*
Benedict's *Rule of St Benedict*
Gustavo Gutiérrez's *A Theology of Liberation*
Carole Hillenbrand's *The Crusades: Islamic Perspectives*
David Hume's *Dialogues Concerning Natural Religion*
Immanuel Kant's *Religion within the Boundaries of Mere Reason*
Ernst Kantorowicz's *The King's Two Bodies: A Study in Medieval Political Theology*
Søren Kierkegaard's *The Sickness Unto Death*
C. S. Lewis's *The Abolition of Man*
Saba Mahmood's *The Politics of Piety: The Islamic Revival and the Feminist Subject*
Baruch Spinoza's *Ethics*
Keith Thomas's *Religion and the Decline of Magic*

COMING SOON

Chris Argyris's *The Individual and the Organisation*
Seyla Benhabib's *The Rights of Others*
Walter Benjamin's *The Work Of Art in the Age of Mechanical Reproduction*
John Berger's *Ways of Seeing*
Pierre Bourdieu's *Outline of a Theory of Practice*
Mary Douglas's *Purity and Danger*
Roland Dworkin's *Taking Rights Seriously*
James G. March's *Exploration and Exploitation in Organisational Learning*
Ikujiro Nonaka's *A Dynamic Theory of Organizational Knowledge Creation*
Griselda Pollock's *Vision and Difference*
Amartya Sen's *Inequality Re-Examined*
Susan Sontag's *On Photography*
Yasser Tabbaa's *The Transformation of Islamic Art*
Ludwig von Mises's *Theory of Money and Credit*

Macat Disciplines

Access the greatest ideas and thinkers across entire disciplines, including

Postcolonial Studies

Roland Barthes's *Mythologies*
Frantz Fanon's *Black Skin, White Masks*
Homi K. Bhabha's *The Location of Culture*
Gustavo Gutiérrez's *A Theology of Liberation*
Edward Said's *Orientalism*
Gayatri Chakravorty Spivak's *Can the Subaltern Speak?*

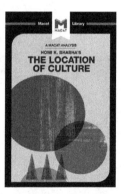
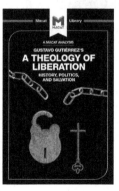
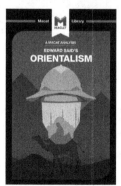

Macat analyses are available from all good bookshops and libraries.

Access hundreds of analyses through one, multimedia tool.
Join free for one month **library.macat.com**

Macat Disciplines

Access the greatest ideas and thinkers across entire disciplines, including

AFRICANA STUDIES

Chinua Achebe's *An Image of Africa: Racism in Conrad's Heart of Darkness*

W. E. B. Du Bois's *The Souls of Black Folk*

Zora Neale Hurston's *Characteristics of Negro Expression*

Martin Luther King Jr.'s *Why We Can't Wait*

Toni Morrison's *Playing in the Dark: Whiteness in the American Literary Imagination*

Macat analyses are available from all good bookshops and libraries.

Access hundreds of analyses through one, multimedia tool.
Join free for one month **library.macat.com**

Macat Disciplines

Access the greatest ideas and thinkers across entire disciplines, including

FEMINISM, GENDER AND QUEER STUDIES

Simone De Beauvoir's
The Second Sex

Michel Foucault's
History of Sexuality

Betty Friedan's
The Feminine Mystique

Saba Mahmood's
*The Politics of Piety:
The Islamic Revival and
the Feminist Subject*

Joan Wallach Scott's
*Gender and the
Politics of History*

Mary Wollstonecraft's
*A Vindication of the
Rights of Woman*

Virginia Woolf's
A Room of One's Own

Judith Butler's
Gender Trouble

 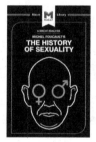  

Macat analyses are available from all good bookshops and libraries.

Access hundreds of analyses through one, multimedia tool.
Join free for one month **library.macat.com**

Macat Disciplines

Access the greatest ideas and thinkers across entire disciplines, including

CRIMINOLOGY

Michelle Alexander's
The New Jim Crow:
Mass Incarceration in the
Age of Colorblindness

Michael R. Gottfredson
& Travis Hirschi's
A General Theory of Crime

Elizabeth Loftus's
Eyewitness Testimony

Richard Herrnstein
& Charles A. Murray's
The Bell Curve: Intelligence and
Class Structure in American Life

Jay Macleod's
Ain't No Makin' It:
Aspirations and Attainment in a
Low-Income Neighborhood

Philip Zimbardo's
The Lucifer Effect

Macat analyses are available from all good bookshops and libraries.

Access hundreds of analyses through one, multimedia tool.
Join free for one month **library.macat.com**

Macat Disciplines

Access the greatest ideas and thinkers across entire disciplines, including

INEQUALITY

Ha-Joon Chang's, *Kicking Away the Ladder*

David Graeber's, *Debt: The First 5000 Years*

Robert E. Lucas's, *Why Doesn't Capital Flow from Rich To Poor Countries?*

Thomas Piketty's, *Capital in the Twenty-First Century*

Amartya Sen's, *Inequality Re-Examined*

Mahbub Ul Haq's, *Reflections on Human Development*

Macat analyses are available from all good bookshops and libraries.

Access hundreds of analyses through one, multimedia tool.
Join free for one month **library.macat.com**

Macat Disciplines

Access the greatest ideas and thinkers across entire disciplines, including

GLOBALIZATION

Arjun Appadurai's, *Modernity at Large: Cultural Dimensions of Globalisation*

James Ferguson's, *The Anti-Politics Machine*

Geert Hofstede's, *Culture's Consequences*

Amartya Sen's, *Development as Freedom*

Macat analyses are available from all good bookshops and libraries.

Access hundreds of analyses through one, multimedia tool.
Join free for one month **library.macat.com**

Macat Disciplines

Access the greatest ideas and thinkers across entire disciplines, including

MAN AND THE ENVIRONMENT

The Brundtland Report's, *Our Common Future*
Rachel Carson's, *Silent Spring*
James Lovelock's, *Gaia: A New Look at Life on Earth*
Mathis Wackernagel & William Rees's, *Our Ecological Footprint*

Macat Disciplines

Access the greatest ideas and thinkers across entire disciplines, including

THE FUTURE OF DEMOCRACY

Robert A. Dahl's, *Democracy and Its Critics*
Robert A. Dahl's, *Who Governs?*
Alexis De Toqueville's, *Democracy in America*
Niccolò Machiavelli's, *The Prince*
John Stuart Mill's, *On Liberty*
Robert D. Putnam's, *Bowling Alone*
Jean-Jacques Rousseau's, *The Social Contract*
Henry David Thoreau's, *Civil Disobedience*

Printed in the United States
by Baker & Taylor Publisher Services